YOUR HOUSE
YOUR CHOICE

WHOEVER TOLD YOU THAT WHAT
YOU DON'T KNOW WON'T HURT
YOU, SURELY WASN'T TALKING
ABOUT YOUR <u>OLDER</u> HOUSE

Hope!
Mommy said you'd
probably need this
prove her sight
before her.
Lasa. Good to see you.
/Re'

RE' PETERS

COURONNE PUBLISHING
WINNIPEG, MANITOBA

Couronne Publishing Inc.
Info@couronnepublishing.com
www.couronnepublishing.com

Book Cover by: Vanessa Mendozzi
Front Cover Image by: Jubril Idowu

Ordering Information:
Quantity sales. Special discounts are available on quantity purchases by corporations, associations, and others. For details, contact the "Special Sales Department" at the address above.

YOUR HOUSE, YOUR CHOICE –Re' Peters -1st edition.
ISBN 978-0-9948637-7-5
Printed in Canada

Contents

I would like to take this moment to dedicate this book to quite a few people. I am grateful to and for family I met at birth and grew up with as well as the family that I got to meet on this journey we call life. You have all helped me grow and I thank you. To my three sons, Daddy is proud of you infinitely. To my wife, you are an amazing woman. God bless you.

Hello and thank you for picking up this book. Your investment in the valuable information contained within helps far more people than yourself:

I have chosen to donate 100% of the net proceeds from the sale of the first half a million copies to The Salvation Army. What this means is that you will not only be helping yourself, but you will be helping The Salvation Army help the poor and homeless in Canada to get back on their feet. This is my way of giving back and if you help this cause, I in turn offer you my expert advice in this book. It will help you with your older house.

Thank you.
—Re' Peters

Your Biggest Investment

Some choices in life are more difficult than others. When it comes to your living situation, a change, even for the better can seem daunting. It's not too often that you or anyone in fact, makes a decision as big as one about your house. Being informed about all aspects and choices available makes it easier to discern the option that best fits your unique situation.

I'm guessing that by now, you may have heard someone say that your house is your biggest investment. What that means to me is that over the years, you've invested time, some effort and maybe even money on this place. Surely you give your house more importance in your mind than you would an ATV or a car. In an older house especially, small aesthetic jobs can quickly turn into huge renovations over time. The problem is not so much the little things that you see but instead, the issues that may be silently growing in plain sight due to lack of knowledge. The nature of such problems are often insidious because you may not know about them until they are far gone. You see in life, there is always change around us and life can get in the way and it can be easy to overlook minor issues as a result.

The information in this book will guide you as the owner of an older house. With my hands on experience since 2008, every single person that I have come across has had a similar story to one of the two I will share with you shortly. As a professional, I guide people through the process time and time again, finding out exactly what drives them and how they are ready to proceed. With the right tools and a knowledgeable advisor helping you through the interconnected steps and requirements, you can get to your end result whatever that may be. To get the most out of my guidance in this book, it is important for you to understand which type of house owner you can relate to. Pay close attention to which story most fits with your feelings and circumstances. This will allow you to proceed with confidence.

A Tale of Two Homeowners

For the sake of privacy, I have changed the actual clients' names.

The first story I want to tell you is about Louise who lived in a house that was in her family since she was a kid. It had been passed down from her parents when they got too old to manage the place. Louise went to the school down the street and she knew about every neighbor on the block or she at least knew part of their story when they moved or the family that had lived there before. Every room in her house had stories and memories. Her older brothers used to tear around the house and practice hockey slap shots in the basement. Anyone with boys knows they can be hard on the walls, floors and fixtures. Her mom struggled to keep them from going wild and her dad was the old school type, who would say:

"Boys, listen to your mother"

Then he would go back to reading his papers or whatever he was doing. As everyone got older the boys moved out and her parents, in their advancing age, started having mobility issues so it was up to Louise to keep the place up the best she could. They finally had to move her parents into an accommodation for elders and it was only after she came home from the first day of them going into their new living space that she actually took it in:

"I walked into the quiet house and immediately noticed that dad's chair by the TV was empty. I didn't pick up the aroma of any meals or baking coming from the kitchen and that's when I felt it very strongly. It hit me...This is it! Everyone's moved on." Louise said.

The emptiness also allowed her to notice many of the little things that she didn't see before because she was focused on her interactions with the people that made this place a home. The ceiling in the living room by the front window had a stain from water damage, the kitchen even though functional was thoroughly dated. The carpet around the house really showed the age of the house. Louise was ready and very determined to bring this place back to and even better than what it was when it was filled with laughter and excitement from her family living there through all the years. Louise reached out to me for advice about doing the obvious renovations like the roof and windows and all that. It was clear that Louise was determined and able to take on the project through to the final step; she had a year off from work, she had lots of funds available to her for renovations and she was ready for guidance. She handled the contractors, the suppliers like a pro (with me being her proverbial angel on one shoulder) and when she was done, she decided to put the house up for sale. Because she followed expert advice and professionally staged the house when all the work was complete, two families fell in love with the house at the same time and they both wanted it so badly that they drove the price up $20,000 above the price that Louise wanted. In case you were wondering, Louise was what I would call an overseer homeowner. More on that later.

The next story is about a previous client we'll call James. He owned a house in the city where he and his family had lived for oh about fifteen years if I remember correctly. James and his wife bought their house when they had their first baby and life just got busy. When they started out, James and his wife had bought the house in a state where it needed a few repairs here and there: nothing major, just maybe some windows here and there and they were going to get around to maybe redoing the kitchen and some new flooring. These were projects they could tackle one at a time, when they weren't too busy with other stuff. Now as time went by, James started some renovations around the house (and with some renovations, you have to tear out the old stuff and often find surprises underneath). He ripped out the old bathroom and put in a pocket door and he also replaced the front door to the house with a really nice, solid door with a built in stained glass window. Oh and James had also started to rewire the house by himself (notice I said started and let's not go into why he would do this without any prior electrical experience, or required permits and inspections). All these renovations were half started all throughout the house meanwhile his family gradually grew to include a few other kids and pets.

At this point, James had a larger family and life just sort of happened you know? He struggled to complete all the work because the list of tasks just seemed to be endless. He also had to always decide which of these things he wanted, to take up his time: work, his wife and kids or trying to finish these renovations which seemed to be increasing. Keep in mind; he had kids who happened to be fairly active. With kids being kids, they are bound to break something here or stain something there. As I write this, I'm listening to my sons and thinking how their normal day involves jumping, thumping, climbing and all that craziness. The other day, they were playing hide and seek and one of them went to hide behind a curtain in the living room. While he waited, he spun around so that the curtain wound up around him and then he tripped because he was wound up and he sort of took the curtain as well as the curtain rod with him. So now, I have a curtain rod with a lean to one side at least until I fix it. What are you going to do? Kids will be kids.

Well that's how it went for James who was trying to fix the place himself but after a few years, it was beginning to really weigh on him just as anyone who lives right in the middle of a renovation can tell you. I mean typically, you can manage at first but after a few months or in this case years, you start to ask things like:

> "How long will it be till I can actually use my bathroom and actually feel proud of it again?"

James had tried the DIY route and he just didn't have that kind of time anymore. It was eating time away from his wife and kids, causing arguments as they had to live around unfinished projects. He could have hired contractors as well but then he'd have to manage people working on his house while his family lived in it. He'd also have to come up with thousands of dollars because well, contractors have families to feed right? James had finally decided that he was ready to find a simple solution to his current needs. James was what I refer to as a handsy homeowner then transitioned into a solutions owner. Again, I'll explain these terms in a little bit.

Regardless of which of these types of homeowners you identify with, there is advice for you here. I remember when I first started learning to drive a car at about age sixteen or so. It was a blue Toyota sedan with a manual transmission. Before I got behind the wheel (and especially when I knew that it was going to be my turn shortly), I would imagine how overwhelming and scary it would be: from the steering wheel not staying straight, to whether or not I would push too hard on the gas pedal or even successfully switch gears. Of course for the first little while I kept stalling the car because, if you've driven a manual transmission car before you know that you have to make a smooth transition between the clutch and the accelerator, or the car will jerk and stop abruptly. After I got out of my own head and started to actually listen to my instructor, who was sitting beside me, all my worries were no longer an issue.

There's really no need for you to feel overwhelmed about your house if you do. In this book, I will be your instructor and by the time you're done reading, you will be able to identify what's going on with your house if anything. You will also get to decide which of the options you wish to take in handling your house and most importantly you can make that decision with such confidence, it would be like you've done this before. Depending on what type of homeowner you identify with, your house as your biggest investment can be handled without undue stress, time or cost with a simple solution to fit your personal circumstances. It is important that you read every chapter of this book as you don't want to miss a section that would be very helpful to you in one way or another. It is your house and it is your choice...on becoming well informed.

Do You Know Where Your House Is?

Sometimes as I go about my day I easily forget to eat lunch or maybe manage to get just a drink of water and then sometimes, say at the end of the day or something, I look into my kids' eyes and I think to myself:

"Once I was a kid. Running around without a care".

They just simply remind me of the cycle of life. We are born as helpless babies, we learn to walk and be autonomous all the way through to our teenage and young adult lives, and then when we get much older, some of that autonomy is lost due to the normal aging process. It's just the nature of things. When it comes to your house, it was new at one point but times have changed and depending on a few factors, it's not only aging but it may need your attention. I will help you understand how the different components of your house age over time so that you can identify and manage the things that speed up the aging process. I believe that just as different stressors in life can age us faster, there are things that if left unattended in your house, can really speed up that aging process so let's get into it.

Your Foundation

The foundation of your house is one of the most important components of the structure as it holds everything else up that allows for you to go about your everyday business. Depending on when your house was built, your basement would have been made by the building methods that were common at the time.

Foundation styles include:

• Slab foundation

• Crawl space (many times in addition to a retaining wall)

• Full basement with or without piles.

These foundations would have been built with either wood, concrete that was poured in place (sometimes with concrete footings and sometimes without) or large stones that were held together by mortar. Obviously some foundation materials and styles are better able to withstand the elements than others and even if the foundation withstood it for many decades, time can still get the best of a foundation if neglected.

Let me ask you. What is your house sitting on? I know it's sitting on the foundation, but what is the foundation of your house sitting on? Soil right? The number one cause of foundation problems in houses is in the soil. So depending on what part of the country you are located in, the soil has a few possible compositions. I know that where I live now, the house was built on a clay soil and clay (as with most other soil types) typically expands when cold and/or wet and contracts when hot and/or dry. Many times, the soil around a foundation moves for many reasons including presence of moisture or a lack thereof. Now I want you to imagine a foundation wall built six, eight, ten feet below the ground with four walls and then over the years, all the soil on the outside of that concrete or stone wall has been moving. Imagine Just how much pressure is being placed on the walls. Soil movement is something that we can expect unless you decide to completely replace all the soil around your house and within a block radius. I suggest we first understand this whole soil thing and how to manage it instead.

There are other foundation styles, namely slabs and crawlspaces, but for the sake of most of the foundations out there, I will focus on the houses that had foundations walls dug into the soil.

Alright so now that you know what the main cause of foundation problems is, I will tell you just how this issue actually arises and this is where you can learn how to mitigate this. As I'd mentioned before, soils expand and contract and the reason for that is simple: Moisture! Water is a source of life but when it comes to your foundation, it needs to be managed carefully. You see, when there is water left around a foundation it will find its way in. Let me explain.

The foundation of your house is already facing inward pressure from the soil. So if you knew about it would you want to add to that pressure? You see water from outside can get into the soil and make this problem just a bit more difficult over time. Rainwater as an example is responsible for damaging too many foundations for me to give a number. It might seem counterintuitive but when I hear about the foundation of a house having problems, the first thing I look at is the roof. I know that might be a little odd but water that comes from your roof, if not directed properly, would go and sit where? Your foundation walls. Over time, that water soaks into the soil causing it to expand and add even more pressure to your foundation walls. As that happens over time, you may get some hairline cracks here and there on your walls which frankly is not uncommon but then what happens when the foundation wall cracks? To give you an analogy, although I'm not really a car guy, but auto insurance companies usually say that if you have a small crack on the windshield of your car, you should get it looked after because it could easily spread and compromise the safety of your windshield. Now let's consider that in the case of a house's foundation walls. When you start to have cracks and the issue behind the walls is not addressed, it's only a matter of time before the cracks spread and even become bigger (I once helped a lady out who had a foundation wall crack that was wide enough for me to put a chap stick into it sideways.) The issue with a crack in the foundation is that not only could it weaken the wall over time but now any water in that area of the foundation will likely find its way into the house as well.

Sometimes if the water is not able to get into the foundation walls, it will find its way under the foundation floor and cause problems such as the floor heaving, high humidity, mould mildew and other problems as a result of all that moisture. And to think that all that started on the roof of the house right?

Still on this thing about moisture causing foundation problems, if you live right by a body of water, then you should be aware that it's fairly common for your soil to have excess moisture from all that water. Worse still is if there is improper drainage at the base of the foundation. Water can eat away at the foundation regardless of what it is made of. Repairing foundation damage, installing weeping tile or a sump pump, can be costly and intrusive.

Trees around your foundation

Another cause of foundation problems that many people overlook is trees. Trees can add an aesthetic appeal to a house in addition to them cleaning the air and providing shade but they can be a problem (You should hear me complain every time I have to mow the lawn in my yard. I have a few trees that drop acorns and twigs so when I mow the lawn...well enough of my rant). One of the things that many house owners overlook is that trees can possibly cause issues with a foundation wall.

Now it's also a common misconception that the roots of a tree can actually push in the foundation walls of a house but that's really not where the damage to your foundation wall comes from. You see the roots of trees will go wherever in the soil that they need to find water. If they're not getting enough moisture, the roots will go further out to get them (ever notice how a large pine or oak tree, usually gets almost no grass underneath because of the lack of sunlight and moisture needs?) When you have larger trees around your foundation, they will search for water and what normally happens is that they take moisture from their surroundings including the area of that foundation wall thereby causing the soil to shrink and in some really hot summers, it causes the soil to separate right underneath your wall.

Vibrations

Another overlooked issue is vibrations around your house as a cause of foundation damage. I remember that on one of my houses, I had an engineer come out to inspect it and the house was on a corner lot meaning it was the last house at the intersection of two streets. One of the streets saw more traffic than just your normal residential street and the sun at its peak was also right around that very corner and so the house had some bad settling around that area. This happened simply because the vibrations from lots of vehicle traffic, added to the issue of a lack of moisture in the soil from the sun, led to the soil giving way around that area and then when you also realize that the house did not have any underpinning done (piles) when it was built, well the house settled nicely. I have also helped people who had a train track beside or behind their house and the vibrations over time when coupled with issue with the soil's moisture could be a challenge.

One last thing about the aging of your foundation. If you have a stone or wood foundation, it may suffer more because stone foundations after so long may start to have some of the mortar between the stones come loose, and if left unattended could be a big problem with water coming in. Wood foundation walls coming in direct contact with soil will absorb moisture over time. Think about wood rot. Now of course this is assuming that there is constant moisture in the soil that's coming in direct contact with that surface, over decades.

Electrical Wiring

The electrical wiring is what brings power from the city or municipality line into your house. It carries fairly large amounts of electrical energy because it is needed to not only light up the house but also to heat up the place or cool it down in the summer as well as power things up that you need in everyday life around the house. Most people rely on electricity to power most of their devices: coffee maker, fridge, etc. Once again age becomes a factor in figuring out the potential problems with the electrical system in your house.

Over time, the need to update electrical wiring has become imperative especially with the advancement of technology. I remember when I was little and we had one of those tube TV's that needed "rabbit ears" above it and you even had to sometimes wrap some foil paper around the antennas to get clear reception. I'm sure that I may have just aged myself a little in my description but yeah, back then, we needed electrical power but not as much as today. Nowadays in an average house of two adults and three kids, everyone has cell phones, laptops and or tablets to boot. The appliances in the house have become a lot more sophisticated in addition to drawing on so much more power. Then with design advancements, one room has six to ten pot lights whereas back in the day, one fixture was just fine. Our demands for electrical power have increased over the years and in many cases, the power coming from the city or within the house's main panel has not been updated. It's sort of like what my auto mechanic told me once:

He said, "Re', if you don't have enough coolant in the radiator of your car, the radiator coolant serves to cool the engine with all that work it's doing driving you down the highway or to your appointments and back. If you are very low on coolant, your radiator struggles to cool the engine and it will only be a matter of time before your engine overheats and well...let's just say that you could get quite the bill."

Back in the day, the amount of power needed wasn't much and so the electrical supply devices (such as your electrical panel box) did not need to be made to handle a higher capacity. These days, with the extra demand for power, these same old devices may not even have the capacity to give you all the power you need, or worse they may be trying to keep up in which case there may arise a safety issue. More on that shortly.

Electrical panels with breakers

Your electrical panel, if you have one, will be a rectangular box with a bunch of wires coming out of it. This panel is where all the power coming from the city or municipality's power line comes into the house. Most of these panels have a small door that opens up and behind the door are your electrical breakers. These breakers which look like toggle switches are linked to different appliances and fixtures throughout the house. Nowadays most houses have an electrical panel with a 100-amp capacity but in the old days, it was not uncommon for an electrical panel to have only 60 to 70 amps and this was once again because the demands for electrical power were not as much as they are now.

There are two main issues with having just 60 to 70 amps today. The first one is that many insurance companies if they know you have only 60 amps, may not insure your house because of implicit safety concerns. If you already have insurance, they may refuse to renew the policy on that account. Secondly (which ties into the first reason), if your house has all these gadgets but not enough power in the house to support them, then you will be putting too much load on the panel or breakers within the electrical panel. Have you ever had an electrical breaker pop in your house? When this happens, you have a light or an appliance go off and when you go down to the panel to check, you see that one of the electrical breakers is automatically set to the "off" switch. This is a safety feature that was created into the breakers.

The reason the breaker pops in the first place is simply because there was too much demand on that circuit (a circuit by the way is a series within an electrical line). Think of a circuit sort of like the old Christmas lights on a string. Some of the old Christmas lights were designed that if you had fourteen light bulbs on a string and one of the bulbs died out, the whole damn thing stopped working. So a circuit within an electrical line works sort of the same way and typically a circuit can take up to twelve items that demand little energy so things like one light bulb, one switch, one wall plug...those would make for three items on a circuit. There are devices that take up one whole circuit on its own such as a furnace or in some cases, a stove. So essentially when a breaker pops it's simply because something on that circuit was drawing too much power from what that circuit can hold. It could also mean that there was a short somewhere on the line of that circuit which is simply a spark. Plugging in multiple power cords to connect your TV, laptop etc. all on one plug is a sure fire way to overload a breaker.

Electrical panels with fuses

Back in the day, fuses were the order of the day. An electrical fuse functions very much the same way an electrical breaker does; to prevent excess current from going through a circuit. The main difference between an electrical breaker and a fuse is that a fuse simply burns out and needs to be replaced if the circuit is overloaded. With an electrical breaker, if there is too much current, it simply shuts off and you can turn it back on. Fuses for the most part were really not unsafe. It was just the inconvenience of having to buy and replace fuses so often. Imagine you have a favourite show and as you're watching it, it gets to a pivotal moment and then the fuse blows so the TV and PVR goes off. To add to that, you don't have any spare fuses laying around. I hope you can imagine what it would be like if you were in the middle of the Stanley Cup playoffs and you have to go fumbling around for a fuse instead of simply flipping a switch. That was one of the main reasons that fuses were upgraded to circuit breakers. The other reason is simply the issue of electrical load capacity of the whole electrical panel.

Knob and tube wiring

These days whenever a potential house buyer hears knob and tube, it's like they stop breathing for a second. It is becoming common for people to wonder not just the cost to replace but also the safety of such wiring within a house. Knob and tube wiring was the way many houses were wired from the early 1900's till about 1950. It was an acceptable way to wire a house way back then simply because the demands needed by all the gadgets in the house were not that much.

Knob and tube wiring has fallen out of favor because the extra electrical power that flows through the electrical lines and the way the knob and tube wiring was built, could pose a safety risk. I'll tell you how to spot this kind of wiring shortly but the reason this can now be an issue is that the wires were usually wrapped up with paper or sometimes asbestos composed wrapping for the purpose of insulating the wires. Between 1910 and today for example, that wrapping may have deteriorated over all this time from the heat of the extra power going through and now you may start to have exposed wire or loose joints, which are a recipe for electrical fires.

These days many insurance companies would not want to insure a house that contains knob and tube wiring because of the increased risk that house has compared to one without knob and tube wiring. Often people say to me:

"Re' I never had any issue with insuring my house before even though it had knob and tube"

To which I advise them that it wasn't an issue for the insurance companies until they learnt over time from different situations that they've had to address. Upon finding a common issue being knob and tube wiring, they would either refuse to insure the house flat out or they would charge a much higher insurance premium.

Aluminum wiring

In my experience aluminum wiring has a higher level of risk in a house than does knob and tube. Knob and tube still needs to be replaced when noticed in a house but aluminum wiring has its special and potentially dangerous challenges.

Between the early 1960's and late 1970's, the price of copper became too expensive and so builders had to find a much cheaper alternative to wiring houses and so they used aluminum wiring. One of the characteristics of aluminum wiring is that when it gets hot, it expands more than copper does and then it shrinks back. Over time, all that shrinking and expanding causes the connectors of the plugs and switches to loosen up, which leaves that fixture highly susceptible to sparking (electrical experts call this arcing). The major problem is that many of the fixtures today, including plugs and switches, are made with copper connectors. What happens is that people connect a new, nice looking fixture with copper connectors, with the old aluminum wiring. When copper and aluminum come in contact with each other and these wires heat, the aluminum releases something called aluminum oxide and electrical experts call this process oxidation. Well the wires get loose at the connection and if that wire is still live then that's where the risk of a fire is greatly increased. A building inspector once told me that about 20% of house fires in Canada are caused by electrical problems and the number one cause of electrical problems is faulty connections either by poor workmanship or just plain wear and tear over time.

Roof

I was walking past the living room in my house one day while my kids were watching some kids' show and it was on commercials. It was a Salvation Army commercial that used very little words and more visuals to make their point. I don't know if you can imagine this but it depicted a mother having to make a hard choice between feeding her child and providing shelter. The mother peeled open the can of food and as soon as she did that, the roof over her and her kid's head peeled off and when she noticed that, she slowly closed the can back up and on cue, the roof slowly rolled back over their heads then her face fell. I don't know about you but that was a fairly powerful thing to watch and it showed the significance of the roof on a house. Even the dictionary describes the word shelter as a place that provides protection from bad weather or danger.

I hope that you already understand the significance of the roof that is metaphorically and literally over your head. Now let's get into the most common type of roofing and how this can age.

Asphalt roof shingles, the most common type of roofing material, have been around for decades and have been the choice of roofing by most owners because of its lower cost of installation than other forms of roofing such as metal, cedar shakes or tile. As with just about anything exposed to extreme and constant wear and tear (in this case, by nature), asphalt roof shingles deteriorate over time. The usual life expectancy of a roof shingle is between 20 and 50 years but a few factors that cause an asphalt roof to deteriorate faster would be things like:

Weather

Over the years, the weather really beats on asphalt shingles and if you live in an area where the weather can change fairly quickly, it is especially challenging for asphalt shingles as they become prone to cracking and or loosening at joints. In some parts of Canada, the temperature fluctuates between 40 degrees Celsius and -50 degrees Celsius and can drop or climb by 30 degrees in one day. If the colour of your roof shingle is fairly dark, it actually absorbs more heat in the summer and if it's an especially hot summer, it holds so much of that heat in, that it could potentially pass that heat down into your house. Imagine wearing a black fur-lined sweater on a hot summer day compared to wearing a light coloured cotton or linen shirt. The difference in how you would feel between wearing those two clothing materials is similar to what it's like to trap so much heat in your roof.

Heat causes things to expand and the cold causes things to shrink and so in the heat of summer, your shingles expand and then when the winter comes, they contract a bit. That's normally not too bad but after a while it will take its toll, especially with rapid fluctuations over a short period of time. Now if your roof is poorly insulated, then there could arise the problem of having the underside of the roof (inside the attic) sweat, which not only damages the wood structure but also causes roof shingles to curl up. If your roof shingles are curled up enough, then water from rain will find its way in.

Another way that asphalt roof shingles can age is in some houses with enough slope but not a lot of air movement in the attic close to the edge, around where the eaves troughs are. If you have snow build up around the edge and that snow melts, then that water can go underneath the roof shingles and damage the shingles over time. You may also notice evidence of water damage on the inside of your house as well. I will share with you one family I knew, who knew they had roof problems but didn't know how or why. Instead, once a year in the spring they had a bucket in the living room where a steady drip leaked out from the roof above. Their situation was more complex and they had more than one issue. However, because the drip only happened once a year, they forgot about it for the most part and life moved on. They were planning to build a new house so didn't want to spend any money on repairing their current house.

Trees

As we talked about with foundations, you really don't want a tree to be too close to the house. Another reason for this besides what I told you about your foundation is simply because the branches over time will brush up against your roof shingles and that will cause your roof to deteriorate even faster. Remember the family with the leaky roof? Well they lived around so many large, mature trees and 25-year shingles lasted them 7 years, max. You can start to see why they preferred the bucket. Who could afford to have a roof replaced every 7 years? You are better off to keep the trees away from your house structure to prevent the problems from happening.

A commonly overlooked aspect of the roof is the area underneath it. If you have an attic, it needs to be properly insulated. Attics are a space where air should move freely. Normally, you need to have an R-50 value of attic insulation and you should also have the accommodation for air to move freely above the insulation but below the roof deck. Check with your local building permit department as their requirements change. If you don't have proper insulation then not only do you have heat escaping in the winter but in the summertime, you lose cool air and if your shingles get too hot, some of that heat is coming in and potentially staying in your house.

Windows

The windows in your house don't really deteriorate unless they have wood exterior in which case, the wood being subject to the elements over the years, will eventually rot if not properly maintained. All this talk about upgrading your windows over the years, really does have merit. Aluminum windows were very common in houses built before the 1900's and it's not uncommon that you would hear someone say:

"Oh we just put these windows new in the 80's"

And they would still be aluminum, single pane windows. Now aluminum single pane windows were fine back in the day simply because people didn't know any better but today, there are so many advancements in the construction of windows that end up saving you money in the long run. The issue with old, single pane windows is simply that they are very bad for energy efficiency and in some cases, sound proofing too. Now you may have never really thought about your windows being so old and inefficient before because you've always had the same bill from the utility company and it has not gone up by much. You may have gotten used to what you were paying simply because you actually did not even know that you were giving that much more money to the utility companies. Money you could have used for other more important things.

Aside from aluminum windows there are also windows that were built with wood window frames. They were essentially a piece of glass that was framed around with wood and then installed in the opening (sometimes with hinges to allow the window to swing open). These types of windows had pretty much the same issue as with aluminum wiring: severe loss of energy as well as poor sound proofing qualities.

Plumbing

The plumbing within a house ages simply by way of becoming outdated in the materials that were used back in the day. With plumbing, you have two types of lines: supply and drain lines. There is the supply line which transports water from the main city line (which is usually by the water meter in the basement) to all the various water use stations in your house. By stations I simply mean, places where you will be using water like your tub, sinks, washing machine, toilet etc. Then you have the drain lines which take used water and waste away from your house and into the city's sewage line. Supply and drain lines can be made out of different materials depending on when the house was built. The supply lines are usually skinnier than the drain lines. The supply lines used in previous years were often made of galvanized steel while the drain lines were also usually galvanized steel but had a wider diameter and then the plumbing stack which is part of the drain lines, was often constructed out of cast iron.

Galvanized pipes were commonly used in houses built before the 1960's and are actually just steel pipes coated with zinc. Over the years, the zinc (which is a protective coating) wears off and so the exposed steel starts to corrode or wear out and rust but it mostly does so from the inside out. All that corrosion built up within the pipe could also possibly cause there to be lead in the pipes as well. Another thing that could arise from old, galvanized pipes is that the water pressure can get weaker as a result of all the buildup inside the pipe.

As for the cast iron pipes, these deteriorate in just about the same way that the galvanized lines corrode except that this pipe does not only transport water now. It also transports waste typically from your house and sends it to the sewage system. The slight difference in how this pipe corrodes is simply that all that waste can cause something called hydrogen sulfide gas to form and as that oxidizes, it leads to sulfuric acid (I don't know if you've ever had a sort of rotten egg smell coming from your sink either in the kitchen or bathroom or something. That smell is usually coming from the fact that there's some waste gas build up within your pipe underneath that fixture) and this sulfuric acid causes cast iron pipes to corrode over time. One other cause of wear that I've seen over the years is in the movement or settling of a house because of the soil and foundation and how that could put unnecessary pressure on the cast iron pipes which eventually either crack or the corrosion burns a hole through some place on the pipe or at a joint. Now I won't ask you to imagine just what happens when the pipe that carries waste away from your house has a leak in it.

Heating

With the kind of weather we have in some parts of the country, heating a house is simply not a luxury. I live in Winnipeg and I remember in December of 2013, we had some really cold spells and to us yes they were particularly cold but ah well, we kept it moving. Okay when it really gets that cold and I can't speak for everyone but you only want to go out when you really must: work, grocery shopping, etc. Going to say hi to a friend is still on the table but you almost have to first assess whether or not you want to brave the cold and everything takes longer to warm up. There was a story done by CBC that the Manitoba Museum had discovered that Winnipeg's temperature was colder than the planet mars which does not have life on that planet. [1] I think they said it was minus 52 degrees Celsius or something. Simply put, without heat things and people freeze quickly.

Did you know that before the 1800's, heating stoves were used to both cook and heat up a house? They were usually made of cast iron and the heat was maintained by feeding coal into the stove. Some houses today still have heating stoves albeit it may not be the only form of heating in the house. The next systems to be used in heating were boilers. The boiler heating system used low pressure hot water and it sent water through its conduit (pipes) to the different rooms in the house. This was way less messy than using coal to heat up the house not to mention that you no longer had to keep feeding coal into the damn thing to maintain heat. With a stove, you also had to be close to it but with the boiler system, there were pipes that brought the heat to the room you were in. The main issue with the aging of boilers is the main vessel which was usually made of cast iron, wrought iron or in some cases, stainless steel. Not only do these materials age over time and can leak but the real fear with these vessels is if they were covered with asbestos insulation, that could be disturbed over the years and that could lead to serious health issues.

---

[1] http://www.cbc.ca/news/canada/manitoba/winnipeg-deep-freeze-as-cold-as-uninhabited-planet-1.2479967

Insulation

I remember the first house I bought for me and my family. It had many windows which let in a lot of natural light. From an aesthetics standpoint, that was great, until the winter time: we would have draughts from around the windows and we would have to crank the furnace up especially on windy days. This house was originally built in 1910 or so.

Many houses built before the 1900's had poor insulation and it wasn't until after 1930 that fiberglass insulation was used in houses. Before then, it was not uncommon for people to place tapestry to block the draughts from coming into the house through the walls. In some cases, paper shavings and or vermiculite were used to insulate a house, although vermiculite insulation was used more in the attic of a house than the walls. Vermiculite insulation was very good at absorbing moisture and also a good fire retardant (slows the spread of a fire by delaying further combustion). In as much as there were these benefits to vermiculite, I was told by the owner of a remediation company that most vermiculite used between 1910 and 2000 was brought from a mine in the United States which was right next to asbestos and so there is a very high number of vermiculite insulation that contains asbestos. Now asbestos is not inherently dangerous to the health so long as it stays undisturbed. The issue with vermiculite in walls is that over the years, it settles to the lowest possible point inside the walls thereby leaving you with almost no insulation in some areas. Now imagine having some confetti being in a large rectangular box and the box is much larger than the amount of confetti in it. Now imagine what would happen if you were to turn the box on its side. What would happen? The confetti would all fall to one side leaving open space above it right? Well this is what usually happens over time with vermiculite inside the wall of many of the houses built around that time. In the case of walls that were insulated with paper or tapestry, well it's not that they were inherently harmful but can you imagine actually having just paper separating your wall from winds with a temperature of -50 something degrees? Paper of course will deteriorate over time between moisture and just its exposure to changes in temperature year in, and year out.

Fiberglass was not used in houses until about the 1930's and even then, it still wasn't a widely used form of insulation in a house until much later. You see if your house still has the old materials used as insulation, it's not really your fault. It's just simply that, that aspect of your house has become antiquated and with more effective ways of insulating a house, your house is not to today's standards. The trouble is some of these things cannot be seen with the naked eye.

Eaves troughs

The eaves troughs, sometimes called gutters, on your house are actually of far more value than just providing an aesthetic look to your house. The eaves troughs of your house are those channels that are attached to the base of your roof. Their purpose is to collect rain water and move it away from your house because as I'd alluded to in the section about your foundation, water if left unchecked can find its way into your foundation or if you have a basement window with a window well, it may find its way into your house through that as well. It was not uncommon for eaves troughs to be made of metal or wood when plastic or hard vinyl was not as readily available. There were continuous flowing gutters and there were gutters that were connected at joints over a certain length. With the changes in weather, wood gutters rot over time and the old metal ones would simply rust, get bent twisted or broken and wear out. One of the factors that seems to accelerate the deterioration of gutters is the accumulation of junk from the tree leaves over time. Not only do they add more weight on the gutters (causing them to pull away from the house after a while), but it ends up defeating the purpose of having one installed in the first place. When your eaves troughs get clogged, the water just simply goes over the side and straight down to your foundation walls.

Siding

The siding on your house is the exterior part of your house that keeps the elements away from your loved ones as well as yourself when you are sleeping at night, and even during the day too, like a warm jacket. Your siding also serves an aesthetic purpose on your house as it is the most widely spanned surface that can be seen on your house. There have been many types of siding used over the years but a large number of houses used either stucco, wood siding, or vinyl when they were built. Wood siding does wear out with more and more exposure to water from rain or melting snow with the smaller pieces of wood shakes deteriorating even more quickly. Stucco usually wears out from shifting of the house, external abrasion (balls being thrown against the wall or other items knocking into it) or simply from wear on the paint on the exterior due to age. Vinyl siding can bend or break under pressure and over time. It also tends to hide any moisture problems going on in the walls of the house behind it.

Kitchen and bathroom

Now the following two areas of your house that I'm going to touch on are more aesthetic choices although some that I've seen also need things done to them due to poor functionality by today's standards. I'm talking about your kitchen and your bathroom, the two most used rooms in the house. You see, aside from obvious damage from water or visual signs of breakage, your kitchen and bathroom age over time aesthetically. Even if your kitchen still does what you need it to do, it can sometimes look like you just stepped into a time capsule and were taken back in time. What was trending in the 1970's is certainly not in favor of general tastes today just like how men wearing bell bottom pants used to be cool. Don't get me wrong, if you love the really classic look of your kitchen then it is your kitchen. If we were looking at your kitchen as something to reflect the value of your house as your biggest investment, then let's be objective together for a moment. Perhaps here you have wood cabinets with chips on the edges or hinges coming off or maybe you have stains on your laminate counter tops from lots of cooking over time. Pasta sauce always tends to spread everywhere, especially when kids are involved. One simple question to ask is:

"When I look at my kitchen, what year does it take me back to?"

Anything older than 1995 is considered to be fairly old. Even some kitchens that were installed new after that time can still be considered to be old or have other problems to consider. Now a kitchen in a million-dollar house that is old and in pristine shape is considered more of a classic than worn out. That's not what I mean by age. I mean that it has been used a lot and when you walk into the kitchen, you get a good sense that it feels tired. The same goes for your bathroom, what year does it take you back to?

Both of these rooms have plumbing and wiring considerations and flooring should be looked at throughout. Depending on how long you have lived in your house, and how many little feet have stampeded through it, many fixtures will be repaired just as normal wear and tear.

How Do You Protect Your Biggest Investment?

It's one thing to know about how a house might age. But have you actually given much thought to the stage in the aging process that your house is in right now? Right now your house may be solid as a bunker but what if it's not and you thought it was all this time. My goal is to help you identify small signs of aging so that little by little you can tackle anything that comes up. These are things you want to look out for so that you don't wake up one morning and feel like you've been hit by a ton of bricks due to the costs of major repairs.

If you know what to look for to catch problems early, that is at least half the battle. Now I know one of my friends used to tell me long ago, that he didn't really care about going for a check-up with a physician. He would say something like:

"Re'? To be honest, if it isn't broke, there's nothing to fix."

I know that the statement:

"What you don't know can't hurt you,"

Is a good way to avoid problems, but do you really want to wait till it gets to that point before you address things? This is a place that provides shelter for you and the ones you love and you're leaving it to chance?

I remember when I got my first car, it was a 1988 Dodge shadow and I was taking a lady friend to a movie. The pointer for the fuel gauge didn't work so I couldn't tell when the fuel was getting low and I knew that I hadn't put gas in it for a couple of days. Sure enough, the car started to sputter until it finally came to a stop. My lady friend had to help me push the car off to the side of the road until a friend arrived to give me a hand. Luckily this wasn't in the winter time but it was still embarrassing for a much younger me. Needless to say, by the time I got some help, the time for the movie was well passed and the general mood had already switched around and not in my favor too.

You might say to yourself that you will cross that bridge when you get to it, but a gentleman who was a mentor to me, told me once:

> "Re, when a problem is not addressed, it not only stays there but it finds its way into other areas, thereby making itself grow."

I don't know if you've heard this phrase before:

> "A stitch in time saves nine."

Well my twist on that when it comes to your house is:

> "A stitch in time saves nine...up to ninety thousand dollars of sudden needed renovations."

Alright so by now, I trust that you've seen the importance of at least knowing what's going on over your head and what's going on underneath the floor where you and your family sleeps.

Let me hold your hand and help you spot any signs of aging in each major area your house.

How to spot the signs of aging

Roof

I want you to go outside your house right now. You can put the book down. I'll be here when you get back. Actually, why not take me with you so that I can tell you what to look for.

Alright, so go across the street from your house then turn around and look at your house. I want you to look at the roof so that the roof shingles are facing you on their flat end. Does the top of the roof look pretty straight or is there a slant? Does the top of your roof have a high point and then the other sides are sagging? Even if you don't have a roof that's in the shape of an inverted V, as long as you can see your roof shingles, this still applies.

Do you have a tree that has so many branches that are rubbing on your roof shingles? Do the roof shingles look like they are starting to slightly curl up or do they look like they are completely curled up? As you look at the roof deck do you see any kind of sagging going on? The rest of your roof shingles may be fine but is there any curling happening close to the bottom end of your roof, where the roof meets the gutters? Do you see actual loose shingles on the roof or on the ground beside your house?

Windows

When I decide if I will have to replace the windows on a house, I first check to see if it's at least a double pane window, which is simply a second layer of glass that usually helps with the energy efficiency of the house. One quick way I do this is either by putting a ring up against the window or I use a flashlight. The number of reflections you see usually indicates to you if you have a single, double or triple pane window.

> **NOTE:** Now keep in mind, there are really old windows that have the one piece of thin glass and then another one on the outside but they're spaced apart by about a half inch or more. This does not make it a double pane window. A double pane will have both pieces of glass right on each other so that the reflection of your ring or flashlight will come back to you as one reflection or what is sometimes portrayed in some old movies as seeing double or triple.

Most aluminum windows installed in the early to mid 90's are almost always single pane and are inefficient to today's standards of energy efficiency, which now translates to real dollars out of your pocket.

There are some windows that were made back in the day that were double pane but they were sealed and framed in with wood. This left an air vacuum between the two panes and in some cases, they contained argon which essentially helped with keeping the elements outside. When the window seal is broken, you will start to see hazing or fogging which is essentially moisture stuck in between the two or three panes of glass in the window.

Make sure both sides of the window (in and out of the house) are clean so that you're sure that you're not actually seeing moisture from outside of the window and automatically assuming that the seal is broken on your window. If your windows have a wood frame, go outside and check to see whether the wood is rotting around the window ledge. That rot could be compromising the energy efficiency of the window, causing the air vacuum between the window panes to become filled with moisture and that's why you would have the fogging or hazing in a window.

Eaves troughs

When it rains and you look outside your window, do you see the water overflowing from the sides of your eaves trough or gutters? Look at the bottom of the downspouts (which is the vertical piece that directs the water from the gutters down). At the bottom of the downspouts, there should be a joint there where the downspout juts out to take the water down from the gutters and then out and away from your foundation. Go outside again and take a look at your gutters to see if they are pulling away from the house. Do you see any obvious rusty holes at or around the bottom along the length of the gutter? That's a sign that it will leak when it rains. Do you see some greenery growing out of your gutters?

Here's one way to test your eaves trough system if you don't have rain: Get your garden hose and let the water shoot up in an arc over and above the gutter so that it lands back in your gutters (you may need to direct the water to hit the roof close to the eaves troughs and then let it trickle down into the gutters). You could also get an eaves trough cleaning attachment at your local hardware store or Home Depot for cheap. This device attaches to the garden hose and has a curved head so you hold it up and it just dumps the water directly into the gutter and it has a handle and a goose neck, giving you the extra height to get to the eaves troughs without much strain to you. When you let the water run, you can then check for leaks at certain spots or overflowing in some spots.

Check the end caps and the joints for any obvious rusty holes that may be inconspicuous. Make sure you do this throughout the perimeter of your house, everywhere there is an eaves trough attached to your house. If you see a section of your house that does not have an eaves trough system and you're not sure if you need one or not, take that garden hose and let the water shoot up unto the roof just above that area and see if the water will trickle down and fall right through that section. If it does, then you know that you will need to address that.

Look around areas where the eaves troughs meet with your siding: do you see long dark streaks of stain running down that side? That's a sign that some water is running down that side of the house when it rains.

Siding

Alright so, if you have wood siding, you will have to take a look at the outside. Check for any signs of rot from over exposure to water. Rotten wood siding may look a bit warped and the color may look different from the rest of the siding. You can take a pen or something just as hard and poke gently to see just how soft that area has become (you can use this method to test the rot of wood in other areas of your house as well).

Watch out for areas where wood may touch earth. Long term, that's not usually a good thing because carpenter ants, which are the cousins of the termites of the U.S., may get into the wood and they damage the structure of wood long term.

Take this opportunity to check around your windows on the main floor as well as the second floor to see if there are any signs of wood rot around the window trims. Do you have peeling paint? Does your siding have mould and/or mildew on its surface? Are there missing pieces at different places on your siding? Any holes for animals to get into or even holes that are small enough for wasps to crawl in and build a nest?

If your siding is stucco, you should look out for staining from too much water exposure or cracking. Now some cracking may occur as a result of the second coat of stucco being put on before the first coat fully cured (essentially not allowing the first coat to set properly during installation) or if the stucco was installed in unfavorable weather. Sometimes the stucco just may have cracks from long-time exposure to extreme weather conditions, especially if that side of the house gets a lot of wind in the winter. You might see hairline cracks at different spots but not around windows or doors. You might also see some slight warping at different locations on the siding.

Tip: Did you know that most vinyl siding should not be painted? Vinyl siding is installed to allow some movement with temperature changes and if you paint siding, the joints usually get painted stiff and so when the siding tries to move, warping results. In addition to checking for signs of warping, check for signs of mould or mildew on the siding. Usually it looks like a cluster of spots that are either black or dark green and it can either be on a small section or span the entire side of the house. You will also want to check for pieces that are coming loose or have already come loose.

Electrical

Have you ever been walking by an area in your house and heard some buzzing? Next time you do, try to find where that buzzing is coming from and see if you can narrow it down to a fixture or an outlet. Buzzing in an electrical fixture or outlet is usually a sign of a loose connection. Remember when I told you about sparking inside your walls? This is one way that you can tell. If you notice that sound, be glad you did because most electrical fires simply don't give that warning sign.

Flickering lights can also be a sign of a loose connection of that fixture especially if it's not happening throughout the house at that very moment. Look at your electrical outlets and see if there are any dark stains around the connectors. That too is a sign of arcing (sparking). If you notice that you have two pronged electrical outlets, that is very often a sign that you may still have some knob and tube wiring in the house (there is no ground wire to that outlet). You can get a relatively cheap device at Home Depot to check the polarity of your electrical outlets (this device will tell you whether the outlet was wired properly or whether it's missing a ground wire).

Now let's go to the basement to see what we have there shall we?

See if you can get access to see your floor joists for the main floor: perhaps you could remove some ceiling tiles? Now don't take out anything you can't easily put back together especially if you have finished drywall ceilings and not ceiling tiles. Don't want you giving yourself more work than necessary.

If you can, look at the floor joists to see if you have any thick black wiring that runs through the floor joists. What I'm trying to get you to notice is what knob and tube wiring looks like. That type of wire should look like the material covering it is a black or dark brown cloth type material. Sometimes you will see the milk colored porcelain knob or tube. The tube is usually set into the floor joist and the wire goes through it to the next joist. Sometimes it may be active and sometimes it may not be active.

Basically, if you see that wire, you should assume that its active unless of course you follow that wire and you see that *both* ends are a cut off on each side. Other than that, I would assume that it is energized. If I see a knob and tube wire routing into the floor of the house to the main floor, I make the assumption that it is feeding something on the main floor and that it is live. If an electrician removed all the knob and tube, they should have removed the old wire to prevent suspicion of active wires. At the very least, they should have left both ends of the wire visibly cut off so we know that it is dormant. Many times I've had clients tell me that they had completely new electrical done simply because the electrician put in a new electrical panel box. It's one thing to upgrade the electrical panel box from fuses to breakers or upgrading from 60-amp service to 100-amp service but that does not always mean the entire electrical system was completely upgraded.

Aluminum wiring

Aluminum wiring is not always easy to spot in your house. The first question to ask is what year your house was built in? If it was between the sixties and seventies (1960's – 1970's) there is a high chance that there may be aluminum wiring in your house unless of course you know for a fact that it has been replaced since then.

Keep in mind that just because your house wasn't built within that timeframe does not mean that you may not have aluminum wiring in your house. It's just that houses built during this time were almost always built with aluminum because copper wiring was very expensive.

Alright so now that we have the year your house was built out of the way, let's see if we can spot any aluminum wiring in your house. The most obvious way to spot it is for a licensed electrician to open up your electrical panel box or an electrical outlet and they should plainly see some aluminum wiring which is more of a silver tone wire on the end as opposed to copper which is the same color as a Canadian penny.

I must stress this, don't go MacGyver on me and start opening up your electrical panel or outlet. Electrical current is no joke...at all! Wait, did I actually just say MacGyver? Wow...anyway I'm serious. I'll tell you some ways you can check without messing with all that electrical wiring stuff by hand. Go to your basement and let's see what we have there. Look at your floor joists for the main floor and see if you see some rather thick wires. Do you see the words, "Kaiser" or "Alcan" or just straight "aluminum"? Those are very clear signs that it's aluminum wiring.

If you don't see those, check to see if you see the number 12 on the wire. This may very well be aluminum wiring but not always so. You see, the number 12 could mean that it is a 12-gauge wire which is aluminum or it could be a copper wire if it's feeding a 20-gauge wire which is usually used for kitchen ground fault plugs near a water source. My point is that if you see the number 12, then there's a chance that it could be aluminum but that's not a dead giveaway unless you know for sure and I'm guessing you're not a licensed electrician. Actually neither am I but I've done this so many times, working directly with licensed electricians, that I know what to look for and I'm here to help you.

Electrical panel

Have you been noticing breakers pop a lot around a certain area of your house when certain things are on? Do you know if you have a fuse box instead of a breaker panel? If you have a fuse box, it should be fairly easy to spot. It would usually be in your basement and it's a box with some glass looking cylindrical knobs of sorts that have been inserted into the box with the glass (usually clear or slightly colored) end sticking out. If you see that, then you have fuses and usually that also means that you only have 60 amps of power feeding the entire house (remember when I'd told you about that earlier when I was talking about how your electrical wiring ages?)

If you have a breaker panel and you've been having breakers pop fairly often, it could be that your house is drawing on more energy than your panel is able to give you but that may not be the case for sure. It could simply mean that you have too many things or one particular item on that circuit that is drawing on too much power through that circuit. Sometimes you may see it right on the electrical panel and it would say on there, "60 amps" or "70 amps". It would usually say that at the front of the panel toward the very top of the panel or there might be a sticker from that manufacturer that will tell you the capacity of that electrical panel.

Now here's something that I want to share with you based on what I've seen so many times: If you see your hydro meter on the inside of your house next to the electrical panel, there's a chance that you have only 60 amps coming in from the city or municipality's hydro line. Of course the only way to tell is to have your licensed electrician check with the hydro company in your area and verify that.

Foundation

I hope you can appreciate that without a solid foundation, everything that you have in your house, all the weight that is being exerted squarely on your foundation walls, could only lead to some serious problems. Here is how you can inspect your foundation to check for any potential issues.

Once again, start outside and let's work our way in from there.

First look at the sidewalk beside your house, if you have any, or just the ground on the side and front or back and see if its sloping toward your foundation. This would usually cause rainwater to go to the lowest point which would be your foundation wall.

Look at the windows and doors, do you see any cracks at the corners of the windows and/or doors? This is a sign of movement of the house and it generally is an indication of some stress on the foundation and it's more a question of how much stress.

Stand on the front of the house and look along the side of the house and look at the walls of your foundation to see if there is bowing in the wall either inward or outward. This is usually an indication of pressure either pushing the wall in or out and that the wall is starting to have a really hard time holding that weight straight up.

The thing about a failing wall is that it reminds me of the game called Jenga. If you've played that game, you know that you take turns removing pieces. The person who takes the one piece that makes the whole structure collapse, loses. See, the reason I brought up Jenga was to help you understand that if one of the four walls of your foundation fails, it causes the other walls to weaken because they start to overcompensate and they too will start to have problems in short order.

Remember that phrase that I put a twist on? "A stitch in time, saves *nine* up to *ninety* thousand dollars." This is one such example that is befitting of that phrase.

Before I get into the cracks, it's important to be aware that it's not uncommon for you to see some cracks on a wall as part of the process of concrete curing over time. If it's a hairline crack and it doesn't span a very long distance, then it might not be a cause for concern unless it's a crack around the corner of windows and doors. What about cracks? Well there are three main types of cracks on a foundation wall: vertical, horizontal or brick-mortar cracks.

Okay so for horizontal cracks, these are usually as a result of pressure on the wall from moisture in the soil expanding outside your foundation. The kind of shifting pressure that's typically happening in the case of a horizontal crack is usually a sideways one. I want you to put both your hands straight out with both palms facing inward, then with fingers straight out, place one hand over the other so that your left palm is facing your right side and your right palm is facing your left side. Now slide your hands so your left hand and your right hand push in further. This is the kind of pressure that is being placed on that wall with a horizontal crack. The more continuous that crack goes along that wall, the further along this problem is.

Vertical cracks are often a result of the footing underneath the foundation wall failing. The walls stand on a concrete platform of sorts that helps transfer the weight evenly across and over to the piles, if any were installed. This is the footing (at least the walls should have footings, but not all walls have had footings installed at the time of construction). So if the footing isn't holding, then the wall itself is not on an even surface and with soil movement, the weight of the house on that one side could cause it to settle, thereby causing the vertical crack.

Now typically, you would need to see at least two vertical cracks on the same wall to know that it may be an issue with the footing underneath that foundation wall. As for the brick-mortar crack, it would typically look like a step formation of the crack along the brick wall and it goes from the top down. This is caused by pressure and if left unaddressed could potentially let water into the foundation over time.

Okay so you've checked the outside walls. Now look for anywhere that your eaves troughs are damaged or hopefully you've done the water test on your roof and eaves to ensure that you don't have water leaking down into your foundation. If you notice an issue with the eaves troughs as well as the foundation, you will have to address both as the foundation would have developed its own problems bigger than the eaves troughs at that point.

Check for trees that are awfully close to the structure of your house. Their roots will find their way around and under your foundation wall in search of nutrients and in especially dry summers, moisture as well. If they take a lot of moisture from underneath your foundation wall, it could cause settling.

On the inside of your house in your basement (if you have one), in addition to the signs of damage just mentioned, see if there are any dark water spots indicating that the wall is wet (this is of course assuming that the walls are open for you to see everything).

I once had a house where we noticed the drywall was wet but there weren't any signs of water leaking from the main floor due to a plumbing problem and so we decided to take a portion of the drywall off and found that the wall was letting water come in like crazy.

Now I want you to look at the concrete floor of the basement. Are there cracks on the floor? Those may not really be a big deal. If you see areas that are heaving (settling where one part of the concrete is now lower than the other but they used to be the same level at one point) that's an indication that the floor has obviously shifted due to the soil underneath. You may see lots of dark, wet spots on the floor from too much water in the soil underneath coming through. You may also see a bump in the floor which usually means that there is more moisture in that particular area and it could be a problem with moisture in the soil or a broken pipe that's letting more water into that area of the soil and pushing the concrete up.

Plumbing

It's not uncommon for the plumbing in a house to be partially updated whereby some copper or pex is mixed in with ABS or the old galvanized steel.

The first place that I want you to take a look at is under your kitchen sink. What kind of pipes do you see there? Copper is the same color as the Canadian penny and pex is often white plastic and both are usually about a half inch in diameter (they can sometimes be wider but in most applications in a home, they are a half inch). Some old plumbing may have some copper but that would actually be much thinner and that usually means you will have less water pressure coming through your tap/ faucet.

You may also notice your pipe to be a worn out silver tone pipe. That's the old galvanized steel that was used way back. Under your kitchen and bathroom sinks, you would want to look to see if your water supply lines (mentioned in chapter 1) have shut off valves that would stop the flow of water in the event that you have a damaged pipe.

Go into the basement and let's check out the supply lines together. How much of the galvanized stuff do you see? Is it all still connected or is it all somehow interconnected with copper to galvanized steel? What you want for supply lines is either all copper or all pex lines or a mix between those two but not galvanized steel.

Your drain pipes for your kitchen or bathroom should be a black plastic pipe that's wider in diameter than the supply lines but if it's old, it would usually be galvanized steel. Sometimes you may have copper drain lines that takes used water away from the sink and eventually to the sewage. Typically, your lines should have a proper grade, which is a slant to allow for water to flow away from the fixture to the proper drain disposal location as opposed to just staying put in one spot.

Standard codes now require that drain pipes be connected to a vent pipe to send out any sewer gases that arise as part of the draining process. In addition to a vent, your fixtures should have traps, which will always hold a little water but their main purpose is to prevent gases from coming back up into the house. A trap is a U shaped part of the drain pipe and the gases get stuck at the bottom of that U while any excess should go through the vent. Now if your plumbing does not have either a vent or a trap, then I hope by now, you see the importance of having both those features as part of the plumbing in your house for health reasons.

I don't know if you've ever heard of a plumbing stack? Well the plumbing stack is actually for drainage and also your main vent. If you look, you'll usually notice on your roof that in addition to having roof vents, you should also have something that looks like (for lack of a better description) a dormant volcano top? Well, the plumbing stack is the main pipe that all the plumbing fixtures (toilet, sinks, tub) send all their drained liquids to, and that in turn sends all that waste down into your building's drainage, which in turn connects to your city's or municipality's sewage system. This plumbing stack generally works with gravity to push the waste down to the sewer and then the gases would typically go up and out of the plumbing stack roof exit. It not only sends out sewer gases but it also allows oxygen to come in and maintains a balance of pressure for the proper drainage flow. It's important to know that in some cases, you may not have a plumbing vent that goes out through the roof. You may have had a cheater vent installed to vent out into the wall.

Okay, so I've just given you a long spiel about how the plumbing stack and venting works but let's look at the stack itself. Check the plumbing stack in the basement and if you can see it on the main floor, check that as well. See if it's made of cast iron which is a fairly thick metal pipe (usually black) that runs from the basement to the roof. When cast iron pipes start to wear out, you will start to notice what looks like water stains only this time, it will be rusty around the joints.

You may also notice cracks from a failing plumbing stack after all this time. It's actually not uncommon for cast iron pipes to crack after so much corrosion. When cast iron pipes start to crack, it would be fairly obvious and not just a hairline crack. Do you see anything like that?

Heating

The life expectancy of heating systems, whether they be furnaces or boiler systems, is about twenty years from the day they go into use. However, I've seen many cases where the furnace had been in use for much longer than that.

I think of it sort of like a car. Most cars are expected to go just fine for up to one hundred and fifty thousand kilometers before they start to really give problems. Well, the fact of the matter is that there are many cars on the road that are at or above two hundred and fifty thousand kilometers. If you never change the oil in your car, it may not even make it to the one hundred and fifty thousand kilometer mark let alone clock two hundred thousand.

The same goes for your furnace; the key component here is how well it's cared for. A furnace that is never cleaned and clogged with dust particles from pets and such, could easily have a shorter lifespan and need to be replaced much sooner.

Alright, first things first, check for a date on your furnace. You may find a sticker that says date of install (ignore the one that says last date of cleaning). If there's no obvious date of install, then how long have you lived in your house or at least how long have you owned it? Was it brand new when you bought or took over the place? One other way to tell the age of your house is to remove the removable door that is usually around the bottom of the furnace. This door should not be too difficult to remove and so if you're struggling with it, then it's probably not meant to be opened and you should leave it be.

On the inside of the removable door, you should see the manufacturer's name, serial number and if you're lucky (as is the case with older furnaces) you may also see the manufacturing date.

I've seen car ads that say something along the lines of, "has had regular oil changes with receipts to prove it." My question to you is, have you actually had your furnace and/or your ducts cleaned every year? If you are able to remove that removable door, just visually check (don't go poking around in there please) and see if there are any signs of rust in that burner compartment. Visually look at the burner inside that compartment. On old furnaces (and even in some newer ones too) you might be able to see the flame whenever the furnace kicks in. Is it blue or yellow? You want it to be blue and not yellow.

Has your heating bill been going up? Are you having to do repairs on your furnace more often? These are all different signs if added to the age of the furnace, that suggest it's on its way out and it might just be a matter of time. Something you want to check and be sure of long before the cold winter months.

Insulation

The best time to find out about the insulation in your house, without having to remove walls or pay for a thermal scan (that shows heat or cool air escaping) is during the winter. This is for the walls.

To check the state of the insulation in your ceiling, take a peek into your attic. If you see sort of a popcorn looking material, that could very well be vermiculite which could contain fibres of asbestos. This is considered highly hazardous to your health so extreme caution is advised. In Canada, it is illegal to remove asbestos without proper certification and equipment. Contact your local hazardous materials removal to get help with this dangerous job.

If you have fibreglass batt insulation in your attic, check to see how much of it you have. Is it sparsely covering your attic space or is it stacked? If you see batt insulation, how many cross layers do you have? Some batt insulation has such tiny fibres that can actually get into your skin pores and become very, very itchy so don't just move this stuff around without gloves and other proper skin coverings and safety glasses.

By now we've covered a lot about what to look for so that you know what stage in the aging process your house is in. Don't forget, I have a simple checklist for you that you can go download for free at www.re-peters.com/yourhousebonuses. On that checklist, you'll find a summary of everything you need to know to check on different aspects of your house.

Why Bother Checking On Your Biggest Investment

B y now, I've told you about how the different components age in your house. I've also given you advice on what to look out for and that should give you an idea of what stage in the aging process that your house is in as of today. Don't forget to go and download the free checklist that I created for you so that you can go walk through your house and identify these things for yourself just like the experts would if you were to pay them to come and take a look at your place. Visit www.re-peters.com/yourhousebonuses

Now the reason I wanted you to go around and identify these things in your house is to help you become well informed. Perhaps if you understood the gravity of neglecting it, then that might get you to really pay attention. As I'd said before your house is your biggest investment and it would be overwhelming if suddenly, your biggest investment is turning into a nightmare and a money pit. Trust me, I've helped many clients who told me about how this thing that used to be their biggest investment is causing them all kinds of stress because of everything that suddenly popped up. The unfortunate truth is that the house did not suddenly get that way. I don't know if you can relate but this is something that my past clients have told me consistently. I remember a lady described it perfectly to me once.

She said:

> "you know Re' at first I would come home and I noticed a little water stain on the ceiling and I said I would get to it when I had the time. Shortly after that, the stain got bigger but not only that, some water had leaked through and my floors really started to buckle and on top of that my stove broke and one day in my bathroom, I just about near put my foot through the floor because it had rotted out. It was like I had a huge laundry list of repairs. Repairs that were going to cost me real time and money. Neither of which I had extra just lying around, waiting for a renovation project to tackle."

All those repairs that seemed to suddenly pile up, were not sudden. They gradually developed at first out of plain sight and then they grew.

Since 2008 I would say at least 85 percent of the people that I've helped, had a fairly similar progression of things: Starting off with just one thing and then in no time, if ignored, those little things add up and it becomes a big problem. Even in my house. My boys keep bumping into this wall or staining that surface or just flat out breaking something. And of course it's by accident. They're children right? Well I was talking to a guy who is sort of an uncle and he has boys too who are older and he said:

> "Re' you wait till they get older and start bringing their friends over" (as I put my face in my palm).

My point in telling you this is simply that things add up and for the most part it can be the natural progression of you living in the house, causing everyday wear and tear. So do you hold off till you have enough money to just do it all at once or you flat out are just in denial until one day, it's at a point where ignoring it actually affects your livelihood. For the sake of expert advice and keeping you fully informed, I will tell you about the progression of things in your house if you decided that you wanted to deal with it at some point in the future.

Roof

Remember when I'd told you earlier about a former mentor of mine telling me about how problems left unchecked, migrate into other areas? Problems with the roof very often can lead to many other problems as well. You see when I go and take a look at a house and see a rotted floor, my goal is to find out what the cause of that is because the rotten floor is simply a consequence and so fixing the floor alone is more of a Band-Aid solution. The leaky vanity or toilet will continue to happen and that time and money I would have spent on fixing the floor would be a waste. So when the roof is deteriorated, the water will usually get in under the shingles and first start to rot out the roof decking, which is simply that wood on which the roof shingles sit. I hope by now, you can understand just how bad, water can be for a house. When water touches wood, it will start to seep in and not only could that lead to wood rot, but it can also lead to the formation of mould on that wood as well. Now as for rotten wood, depending on the level of slant on your roof, its not uncommon during some winters for there to be lots of snow sitting on your roof and all that snow gets heavy. If the wood holding it up rots out, then that snow really has nowhere else to go but down. Even if the roof deck still holds, you now have mould plus the possibility of that snow melting and letting all that water come into the house.

Remember when I was telling you what one of my clients had told me about things just becoming a "huge laundry list of repairs?" Well it all started from the roof shingles. First the shingles curled then there was some heavy rain and the water got in under the shingles to the roof deck and slipped through. This in turn caused mould around the roof deck and soaked up the insulation in the attic. Now the interesting thing is that all this must have happened for a while before she actually saw that little stain on her ceiling. Only a short while later, some of that water went on to the floor in the living room and her hardwood floors soaked up so they expanded and then buckled. What you don't know doesn't hurt you right? Not in this case. By the time it was enough to warrant my client's attention, she truly had a list. Let's look at the progression here and how one repair turned into several: the roof shingles – roof decking – insulation in attic – drywall in ceiling - complete flooring replacement in that room...wow! I say wow because as I write this to you, I'm really noticing the gravity of this. I've always known to look for the source of a problem rather than the symptom but writing it out just helps me see how this can become overwhelming in a hurry. Instead of fixing the roof once, now she had five or six things to fix and of course the cost of fixing the roof was minor compared to all these other things.

The one piece that I did not mention about a failing roof is if the water compromised the roof structure in the form of the joists. That is what holds up the roof and keeps everything in your house essentially safe from rain, snow, very hot days in summer, wind, all that. I will say that I've helped many people with houses in need of repairs but I have not once come across a situation where the roof structure was completely compromised whereby it caved in but that's not to say that won't be the eventuality.

Foundation

I would go ahead and tell you that more than 50% of issues with your foundation will come from your roof or your eaves trough system on your house and for that reason, I will talk about the dangers of failing eaves troughs all under this area about your foundation. I believe I'd mentioned earlier that whenever I hear that a house has had foundation problems, I immediately look up toward the roof and or the eaves troughs. If the eaves troughs are not doing what they're supposed to (channel any rain or melting snow water from the roof, down the sides and out and away from your house) then the natural place for the water to go, will be right beside your foundation wall and it will seep into the soil around your foundation walls. When soil gets wet, it expands and when it dries up, it shrinks. Expanding soil puts inward pressure on the walls and even if it worked fine for decades, its day may come when it starts to give in. To some extent, when your foundation wall starts to crack and it's a crack that spans the full length of the wall, then it will only get worse assuming nothing is done in the meantime. I once helped out a nice lady who lived just fine in her house for many years and then one day, she saw a pool of water around one corner of her basement. Not only that, she started to have an issue of mice infestations. Well when the wall was opened for repairs, it turned out that the footing had failed underneath one wall and the other wall that was connected and running perpendicular to it was also cracked. I mean that crack was so pronounce that I was able to stick a chap stick in the space between the crack. No wonder mice were able to easily find their way into the house.

There was another couple I distinctly remember, whose foundation caved in on the wall that was just under their son's bedroom. Talk about something not to play with. That wall had no eaves trough and so whenever it rained over the years, it just dumped water around that area of the foundation and because the basement was partially finished, they really didn't notice much until the wall started to bulge in but the bulging devolved fairly quickly from when they noticed to the point where a decision had to be made. The soil had pushed and pushed and pushed. Yes, at the time it would have cost them a little over a thousand dollars to install new gutters and downspouts but they now had to completely replace that one foundation wall, underpin it, waterproof it and then also do some remedial work to a second wall that was starting to have problems from overcompensating. How much did all that cost? More than 30 thousand dollars. I'm not a contractor but did the eaves trough need to still be replaced? Of course it did, otherwise they would have to go through the whole process again. In the end a thousand dollars and a quick eaves trough replacement would have been less expensive and simpler than the major foundation repair.

Electrical

My very first client in 2008 was a lady who had a friend stay at one of her houses. He was slowly fixing the place up while he stayed there and one day when he wasn't home, the neighbors called 911. There was a fire that started in the living room and even though it was put out, the whole house was completely covered in soot (black smoke). All the furniture, fixtures, windows, flooring, all damaged by thick, black smoke.

Electrical fires, one of the most destructive things that can happen in a house, are usually the most silent after water but they are far more devastating because when it gets to the point of raging, a fire consumes just about anything in its path and quickly too. I say it's one of the silent destroyers simply because if you don't know what to look for, the risks may be mounting to a big problem but everything seems fine until it goes ablaze.

Overloaded breaker

Remember when I told you about how electrical ages and if you have a loose connection, you may start to have what electrical experts refer to as arcing? (Which is simply sparking) Well I want you to remember the last time you heard about a wild fire in the forest or something. Especially something that started on a camp ground. It could have started from something so little as a spark sized flame from someone not putting their fire completely out. When you add that to a little breeze stoking that fire, this small spark becomes bigger and since it has dry leaves or other easily flammable things around, it quickly spreads. If we were to bring that within the context of a house, you get a spark on the inside of an electrical outlet and the spark is happening at random times. Next thing you know, it may catch unto some building material inside the wall and just grow from there and the rest I'm sure you can imagine. It's really unfortunate because whenever fires damage a house, they do more than just damage the structures. A house fire affects livelihoods from displacement, uncertainty to emotional and financial stress. All for what? Because someone hooked up too many things unto an extension cord? There was a local story the other day of an apartment building that was being built brand new and somehow there had been a fire that started in the vacant apartment building. The fire not only destroyed the building but it took the houses on either side along with it. The people in those houses got out just in time. According to the news, the total damage was estimated at about 4.5 million dollars. I'm sure that was the damage to property. What about things like travelling passports, photo albums from childhood, an heirloom given by someone passed. Can you imagine the devastation that these people would now have to cope with?

Plumbing

It's very important to be aware of plumbing in your house because there are a few issues that could develop as a result of not having your plumbing in good condition.

Mould: If you have a leak due to plumbing in your house, it generally takes two to three days of constant exposure to moisture for you to start to have some mould forming especially if the material that comes in contact with the water is porous (which basically means that it can hold water) like drywall or insulation. You can have leaky pipes in other places in the house but in my experience, whenever I go into a basement, I automatically know to pay closer attention to my sense of smell. If you go into your basement and there is moisture, you will start to pick up a musty sort of smell. Materials that have mould on them if not removed may spread. You see, mould has spores (sort of spongy looking organisms) which are usually too small for the naked eye but in the presence of moisture, they can reproduce and therefore cover more areas. Exposure to mould can be responsible for respiratory problems in people and pets. I distinctly remember a house I went to see once where this couple lived with three small children. There was mould just about everywhere in the house from a leaky roof and too much moisture in the bathroom but even the kids' room had lots of mould and that's where they slept. Now luckily, they were already moving their stuff to the grandparents' place but I had to look this guy straight in his eyes and tell him that I would be back to check if they've moved and if not, I'd have to do something about it. Sure enough they had moved when I came back to check. After I left that house the first time, I don't know if it was because I knew that little children were sleeping in that or because the air was just so heavy from all the mould (or both) but I actually felt ill. Don't get me wrong, it's not uncommon to see a little mould in bathrooms and around kitchen faucets and those can be cleaned using mould cleaning agents available even at Walmart. That's one thing. If you have more mould than just a little on a surface here and there, then you are at greater risk of respiratory health issues. And that little mould that's on a surface, if you do nothing now, it will spread and then you go from surface mould to needing a remediation company to come get rid of it. In the worst case scenarios, these guys come in with machines to balance the air out and they strip that area all the way down to the studs. EVERYTHING goes. I don't know if you know anyone who has had a mould remediation done but it can be quite a costly project to undertake and it requires specialists with the proper training and certification to deal with if it gets to that point.

Lead

It was not uncommon for service lines coming into a house to have been made of lead up until about 1980 or so. Now even if they have been replaced but you still have galvanized steel pipes, they could have accumulated some lead over the years and when the galvanized steel pipes start to corrode as they eventually do, it could release lead into the water you use in your house. This issue of lead being released into the water doesn't happen too frequently but according to the World Health Organization, it affects children in particular.[2] So even though it might not happen a lot, it just takes the right combination of factors (either existing lead pipes servicing water to your house or replaced lead pipes but still existing, original galvanized steel pipes) for this to become an issue.

Flooding

I've had this almost happen to me once in a house I lived with my family whereby one winter, the kitchen faucet just stopped working. I checked inside the cabinet below to see if the shut off valve for the pipes was off but it was not. It wasn't until I went to check in the basement and found that the

---

[2] http://www.who.int/water_sanitation_health/diseases/lead/en/

supply lines were right up against the foundation wall. There had been a few days of strong winds and so the pipe froze. I was lucky that the pipe did not split because it would have basically flooded my finished basement in almost no time. Now what if something like that happened in your house and on top of that you weren't home because you had to work? Or worse you were on vacation for a few weeks? What would it be like to come home to 3 or 4 feet of water when you open the door to your basement? Such a minor detail as not knowing about having your pipes against an exterior wall in the winter can lead to a flooded basement where not only is the furniture damaged, but the basement would need to be gutted in order to fix the mould growth and water damage.

Heating

Have you ever thought about this? The idea that the air you breathe is very important but for the most part also taken for granted. When you have air in abundance, you don't really think too much of it until there's really thick smoke or you just have a serious shortness of breath. In that moment when you are wheezing, its like nothing else matters. Your heating system is similar during the winter months because it provides heat and you usually don't think about it too much. If it gets a little too warm or too cold what do you do? You simply go to the thermostat and adjust it accordingly right? Its not until you have no heat in the dead of winter that you realize how much you really need that heat.

There was a winter when my wife and kids were sleeping and I woke up to being so cold. I went and checked out the thermostat and it just would not respond. I changed the batteries of the thermostat but that did nothing. Now at this point I'm starting to worry about my kids so we call someone who had some heaters that we borrowed in the mean time to heat the kids' rooms while I called a furnace repair place to come out. After checking it all out, the guy told me that he had to order the parts and they wouldn't come in until the next day even with a rush order. Luckily, I did not have to replace the whole furnace but instead a motor but I asked the guy anyways,

I said:

"what would it cost to replace my furnace right now?"

Repairman;

"to be honest buddy, waiting to replace your furnace during an emergency is not the best for you. At a time like this, you would end up paying almost twice the regular cost because parts have to be ordered on such short notice and technicians charge a premium for their time on such short notice. Besides when we're out there for such a call, a dishonest guy knows that he has you by your balls so you'd go with it anyways."

And on top of that issue of having to pay a crazy price to replace a furnace in an emergency, I also had to worry about pipes first freezing then bursting all over my house because it had gotten so cold inside the house that I had to shut off the water at the main line. Ice generally starts to form when the temperature reaches minus 6 degrees Celsius so in the event your heating system goes off, your pipes would usually start to freeze at about that time. Keeping your furnace clean and maintained is important. Replace your furnace filters often. There are so many kinds of furnace filters: some you need to replace monthly, some you need to replace every 3 months and there are some that you may need to replace monthly but you simply have to wash them and when dry, you can re-install them.

Have your furnace motor and ducts cleaned at least once a year so that not only do you have clean air flowing but also you don't have debris and or dust slowing your furnace down and making it work much harder than it needs to.

Building materials damaging

When a house has been left cold for a while, in addition to potential pipes freezing, things just generally contract and so you may see things like some types of flooring starting to buckle or you may see peeling paint. Now the house would need to have been without heat for quite a while for you to start to see changes like this. I've usually seen this in houses that were vacant for months.

KITCHEN

Cabinets

Alright by now you've at least asked yourself the question, "when was my kitchen installed new?" When you walk into your kitchen tell me, if you were to think of a year as you look at your kitchen, what year would that be? The point of me asking you to do this is to get a feel for just what your kitchen feels like. Do your cabinets look like they could use a good cleaning at the very minimum and a complete overhaul at the most? Is there any obvious damage to your cabinets from looking at it? What about water? Was there ever a leak from a dishwasher or something or overflow from the sink? You want to check for obvious damage to it. Is your countertop chipping in certain places? Do you have stains that are just about impossible to scrub off? Is your sink shiny or has it gone really dull from years of exposure to hard water? What kind of countertops do you have? Laminate countertops are still very much in use today because of their cost effectiveness but more and more people are opting for granite or quartz stone countertops in keeping with the trends of today.

Appliances

One thing that can very easily give away the age of a kitchen is if the kitchen appliances have a bone color to them. They could still be quite functional but overall your kitchen will look aged with older looking appliances.

BATHROOM

With your bathroom, again the main thing with aging of a bathroom is with the look and maybe sometimes the function. Just like with your kitchen, when you stand at the door of your bathroom, what year would come to your mind if you were to give one to your bathroom? This is the general feel your bathroom is giving off to anyone who comes by. Are your tub and toilet green or pink? Look at the bottom of your tub. Is it worn visibly? Do you have mould forming around the area where the tub meets the tub surround or at the base of the tub where there may have been water rolling off the edge? Even your tub surround, how worn out does it look?

Now I'm not saying you absolutely have to do this but if you want to get an idea for what is current for people's tastes, go by these show homes that new house builders have for display. See what the bathroom looks like. The tub, the toilet, flooring, all of it. Your bathroom does not have to be exactly like that but it will give you an idea of what I'm talking about. If you have a green or pink colored tub or toilet, that is really dating it. If your toilet is in a completely separate room than the rest of the bathroom, that is considered to be old style although I would have to say that was a good one for functionality. Claw foot tubs are a matter of aesthetic choice. They are clearly a sign of an old bathroom although some bathroom designs these days incorporate the use of a claw foot tub to give a perfect blend between the old and the new. Tile, flooring and accents are some of the most obvious ways to date a bathroom and also places where you can look for water damage, or damage.

Where to Start?

N ow in order for you to get the best value from all this advice, it's important you first understand exactly what kind of homeowner that you would be classified as. What do I mean by that? I've come to understand that every person who has come to me for advice, was usually one of three types of house owners and you should be able to see yourself as being one of these types of owners when it comes to your house. These are terms that I have simply coined based on my extensive experience: the handsy homeowner, the overseer homeowner and the solutions homeowner. Let's get into these terms that I've used to identify the different clients that I've helped since 2008 as I've done several millions of dollars' worth of real estate.

The Handsy Homeowner

This is a homeowner who prefers to do things around the house by themselves. You take pride in being wholly responsible for whatever the outcome is as it pertains to your house be it renovations or sale or design. You want to handle every step of the process and would rather not leave it to someone else as you possibly feel that no one can do it exactly how you would like. You may also be looking to keep more money in your pocket after all. You take full responsibility: if a kitchen sink leaks, you want to fix it, a room needs new hardwood floors, you take a couple of classes and you do it yourself.

The overseer homeowner

If this is you, you are one who takes pride in being responsible for an outcome as it pertains to your house but you may not have the time and in some cases, expertise to handle it so you are okay enlisting the services of a professional. Even with the help of a professional, you may still micro-manage the process after all you want to make sure that the outcome is exactly to your liking. You likely don't look at hiring a skilled person as wasting money but rather, leveraging your limited time and also limited skillset in some cases. You hire a landscaping company because you want your front yard to look just like that one you saw in a house magazine but you'd rather someone who does it every day than you who will be doing it for the first time. You know exactly what it is that you want it to look like but because of your limits on time, you get someone else to bring that to life albeit you are with them every step of the way.

The solutions homeowner

This type of homeowner is one whose primary focus is on the final end point. You may not have the time or all the resources to micro-manage it all or even be completely handsy. You may have been a **handsy** or **overseer** homeowner at one point but you've found this not to be a good fit for your circumstances and so you are ready to move on. You would rather have someone who is proficient at it to handle it all the way and you just want to see it at the end. As an example, if your car has an issue with the radiator, would you do it yourself or look over your mechanic's shoulder or just let them do it and once its fixed, they can tell you what they did? If you said in your mind that you would rather they just fix it and tell you later, then in that car scenario, you were in the solutions mindset.

Now what I find interesting is that we all have these different traits in us and depending on the situation, we will be in one frame of mind or the other. Take for example if you had to deal with a legal matter that was fairly complex and you hired a lawyer. My inclination is that you would be in the solutions frame of mind whereby you want your lawyer to handle it and keep you in the loop: your lawyer will tell you about the big picture of each step of the process. You wouldn't want to go through the 650-page document for this transaction after all, isn't that what you're paying your lawyer to do? Now you may be the very same person who would switch into a handsy mind frame person when it comes to something like doing your personal taxes or something that you have confidence in. Of course some people will be in the handsy mind frame in this legal scenario of reading every line on a 650-page legal document. You see my point? Okay so I want you to be aware of those three mind frames (handsy homeowner, overseer homeowner and solutions homeowner) as it pertains to your house and then based on which one you identify with, you can decide what's the logical step for you to take control of your house.

Remember the story I told you in the introduction about Louise and James in the Tale of Two Homeowners? Well, Louise was an overseer owner because she essentially supervised all the contractors, the suppliers, deliveries, all of it. She micro managed the project to completion. James had tried his hands on being a handsy homeowner by starting several projects around the house and when he realized that it was taking him away from his family, he transitioned into being a solutions homeowner.

Up until now we have gone through a lot about your house from the aging process, how to determine what stage in the aging process your house is in and even what could happen as a result of these issues progressing over time. Remember I told you that your house is one of, if not the biggest investment you will ever make and you know by now that aging will happen whether you like it or not.

Let me ask you something. Is there something that you could physically do say, ten years ago that you can't do right now? Maybe you could still do it but it would be with greater effort? An older friend of mine told me once about how as you get older, there are just things that you cannot do like you used to. It's like things get taken from you as part of this thing called life. Even I can attest to that. Time can do that to you, me or anybody even when we take care of ourselves so what about your house? You see the bottom line is that if you don't take care of your house, that thing you think is an investment will lose its value and depending on how badly it depreciates, the value would have to be significantly reduced in some cases, down to just the value of the lot. As a matter of fact, in some cases an empty building lot with no house on it can be valued more than one with a house that needs to be torn down because you still have to come up with thousands of dollars to tear down an old house on a building lot. The truth is that you can choose to manage your house and its upkeep every so often in small bits and pieces; otherwise you will inevitably get to the point of having to come up with tens of thousands of dollars to correct any disrepair unless of course you chose to go with the simple process. If your house gets to the point of significant disrepair, someone will have to come up with the money to bring this house back so now the question is, will that someone be you?

Now I'm going to give you some advice on what you can do often, if your house hasn't gotten to the point of needing lots of renovations. Regular maintenance, can prevent some of the more severe, costly repairs and problems. If your house is past the point of no return of the aging process, that's okay too because I have some advice for you on how to go about it in a little bit okay...Good.

Regular maintenance

Listen. When it comes to the maintenance of your house, there are some things that you can do and there are some things that I would advise you not to bother trying to save a buck because the risks are just too great. Even if you identify as a handsy homeowner, you wouldn't want to rewire your house on your own simply because an electrician gave you a quote you thought was ridiculous would you? I hope you said you wouldn't and if you said that you would, well that's on you but it is seriously not recommended. Unless of course you are already a licensed electrician then hey, good for you! I will give you some advice on how to go about hiring the right person for the job and in some cases, you may save money in the process but more on that later. Okay so for the maintenance, let's start on the outside of your house and work our way in.

> DISCLAIMER: All advice given here is for information purposes only. Any choices you make based on this information are yours alone. There is no liability on my part for things you choose to do yourself. I'll leave that decision up to you and as adults; your decision to hire someone or to do it yourself will fall squarely on your shoulders.

Roof

For your roof, there's not much you can do for when your roof shingles have started to curl but you can check around for any tree branches that may be close to your roof. Those will wear your roof shingles out much faster from constant brushing up against the shingles when there's a wind. In the winter time, you want as much as possible to clear off any sitting snow that's hanging close to the edge of your roof otherwise you may get ice damming which ends up getting some water to back up and eventually show up on your ceiling.

> **Here's a tip:** You can get something called a roof rake to clear snow off your roof but it's best to try and get it from your hardware store

during the off season. If you need a roof rake in the winter when everyone else needs it too, chances are that the hardware store might be out of stock. Another alternative that people spend a little more money on is roofing heat cables. These things are usually set up on the roof closer to the edge where that ice sits and whenever there's a bit of snow, these heating cables simply melt the snow off and your problem is solved. Obviously the roofing rake is cheaper not to mention that you probably would have to pay someone to setup the heating cables if you don't do it yourself.

Eaves troughs

For your eaves troughs, you want to make sure they are always kept free of debris: usually leaves. You can clean them after the winter as all the falling leaves from the fall won't likely stop until winter time. You will need a device sometimes referred to as telescoping wands, which you can get at Home Depot and you simply explain to them what you're trying to do. Basically it's a wand that connects to the end of your garden hose and it allows you to reach all the way up into the gutter system to flush out any debris sitting in there and allow for rainwater to flow properly down and away from your house. If the debris is stubborn or really caked up, then someone may have to go up there and clean it out.

If you don't want to have to worry about doing this, every year, you can spend a little more and get gutter guards. These things are installed inside or just above your gutters and they prevent leaves from getting into your gutters in the first place. You can also check any hardware store for these. They need to be properly installed in order to do what they're designed to do so either read the directions, or have a qualified professional complete the install. Oh and don't forget to make sure that your downspouts are properly connected from the vertical piece to the horizontal piece to lead water away from your foundation. If you must, you can get downspout extenders to take the water further out and away from your foundation walls.

Siding

With your siding, it's often a good idea to clean it whenever you begin to notice a buildup of dirt and or mould spores. A good pressure wash with soap and water should do the trick. One thing to be mindful of though is that paint made before 1960 and up until 1978 may contain lead which is not safe for you or your neighbor's health so be aware if you decide to pressure wash your siding. You don't want paint chips that contain lead to get blown out into the air.

Foundation

Okay so with your foundation, you want to walk around and see if you have any trees that are close to your house. Typically, a tree that is two feet or less away from a foundation wall should be of concern. Even two feet is awful close especially if its a nice, mature tree. It provides shade but that benefit is completely eclipsed by the potential problems it can cause to the soil thereby affecting the foundation. My advice to you is to have that tree or trees removed. If the tree is very tall, please hire a professional arborist. The extra money is worth the safety in knowing the tree will not accidently fall on power lines, your house, vehicles or people. For the unexperienced person, cutting a tree down is not a simple task and can be very unpredictable.

Next you want to see if on any of the four sides of your foundation, there is a slant going toward your foundation wall. I've seen many times how the paving stones on the side of the house settle over time thereby creating a slope into the foundation. You would want that addressed so that you don't have water going toward your foundation. Many times, people have quarter down (little rocks that compact when wet) installed to create a slope and that slope rolls any water coming down the side of the house, a little bit away from the foundation. Regardless of what you use, the land must be sloped away from the house.

Now this is one part that I will have to almost contradict myself on. Remember when I told you that water can be one of the worst enemies for your house? Water can be good for your foundation sometimes. Let me explain: You see the problem with water and your foundation is that if there is too much in the soil, the soil expands and pushes in on your foundation walls from the outside or your foundation floor. If there is not enough water in the soil, then it dries up and separates which would in turn cause your foundation to settle in different places. You see, there have been some summers that have been very hot and dry. So much so that it started to cause problems with foundations left, right and center. I helped a couple once and they told me that they'd built their house brand new in 1963 and never had a single problem with the house until one year in about 2013 when all of a sudden, one side of the house sank. I hear things like this a lot:

> "I've lived here for over 3 decades and I've never had a problem with that"

Well in that one year, it had been so hot and dry that the soil underneath the house contracted and whenever that happens, it does not contract evenly so the house settled. If you want to see signs of a really dry soil, simply look around a park or somewhere there is soil. If you see lots of what looks to be cracks in the soil, then you know that the soil is dry.

Okay so let me tell you how water can be of benefit to your foundation. Whenever you have a summer that is very hot and you can tell that its dry, you would want to look into getting something called a soaker hose. It looks like a regular garden hose except that it has some tiny holes all over so when you connect it to your garden faucet, it will release water in little trickles. I know I know, I said earlier that you don't want water around your foundation. Well you don't want too much or too little water in the soil around your foundation. You will only usually need a soaker hose when you know that it has been an especially hot summer and there's not been a lot of rain. You can get the soaker hose at your hardware store and again you might want to get it during the off season because if you decide to go after the weather channel has forecasted a whole week of +30 something degree Celsius weather, well so is everybody else at that point. You would want to place the soaker hose about 12 inches or so away from your foundation wall and then leave it running for 20 minutes at a time for about 3 times a week. I want you to listen. If you already have obvious cracks in the foundation like the one I told you about earlier where I said that I could fit my chap stick into the crack, wetting your soil may not be a very good idea. With the soaker hose you shouldn't really have enough water in the soil to make the soil expand. The point of this hose is simply to keep the soil moist so that it doesn't contract.

If you have some cracks on the inside of the basement, you can have some hydraulic cement (sometimes called dry patch) placed over the crack to prevent any seepage depending on how bad it is. Now having said that, you won't be doing much good if you haven't addressed the cause of the problem in the first place. Many times I see people's foundations where they tried to patch up a crack on the outside but for one, a trained eye can tell that it was a patch up job and secondly, patching up the crack without addressing the source of the problem will only lead to (and I've seen this countless times) the crack breaking through the patch and the problem persisting and getting worse than it was before.

Here's one for you. If you have lots of trees in your front yard, you may want to consider having a licensed plumber coming by every couple of years to clean up your line between your house and the city's sewer line. Trees in your front yard can be notorious for having their roots get into the line and clog the flow leading to a potential back up in your basement. The main undiscovered issue I wanted to point out is that if trees do that severely enough, you may have the pipe under your basement floor deteriorate and then you could have water underneath that floor thereby leading to heaving and other foundation problems.

Windows

For your windows, if they're really old, there's not really too much you can do with them besides cleaning them regularly and then constantly checking to make sure that the seal is still intact. If you have old, aluminum single pane windows or just generally energy inefficient windows, you may want to consider thermal window films. These are purported to give your window a little more energy efficiency by preventing cool or hot air escapes depending on the season. In some cases, they may also protect your house from rays coming in from the sun. Using window films has nowhere near the same energy efficiency as a proper dual pane (or more superior), argon filled window.

Plumbing

Let's talk about some things that you can do to prevent your plumbing from becoming a major cost or headache to you. If you don't have any cast iron or galvanized steel pipes, great. If you do, I would advise you to update them as soon as you are able. Have you ever noticed your copper or pex supply lines leaking in the summer time where they're just wet? What I want you to do if you see that in the summer time is to wipe it completely dry and see if you still have water immediately seeping through. If there is still water immediately then you have a leak. If you don't have water immediately then your pipe is experiencing a common term used by plumbing professionals called sweating. Your supply line sweats when the water in the pipe makes the pipe much cooler than the temperature in the room outside of the pipe, leading to condensation. If you notice that you have sweating pipes, you can simply get pipe insulation at your hardware store to wrap around your cold supply lines that are experiencing this sweating phenomenon.

When you notice the temperature outside getting cooler, you should turn on the shut off valve for your garden faucet and let all the excess water completely drain out before shutting off the faucet. You do this because that faucet is usually on the outside of your house while the plumbing line comes all the way into your house so you don't want to risk too much cold causing your line to freeze in the winter time.

You know how you had checked to see if your supply line was sweating, you may want to consider checking all the lines visible in your house to see any obvious signs of leaking such as water pooling around an area or the pipe being wet at the joints. If you notice your water bill being higher than normal and you're sure that you're not using any more water, go ahead and shut off the water at the main shut off valve where the water comes in from the city and see if your meter still moves after that. You may have to wait a little bit or go do something else and come back to it. If it still counts even when it's off, then you have a leak on the line and you can call a Plumber to look into it.

If you have cast iron or galvanized steel, you may notice what looks like rusty water stains around your pipe but check closely to see if there are any cracks in the pipe itself. When these really age, they can crack.

One that is often taken for granted is the flow of water through your pipes. You want to make sure that you use some sort of drain flushing mixture to flush the drains of your house from your toilet to kitchen sink to bathroom sink and tub etc. If that's not done and your house is like mine where my kids are all running around with manes, you'll have hair in those lines which will cause clogging over time. This solution doesn't have to be anything fancy, I've used a brand called Drano from Home Depot and at one point, I even used oxygen bleach which is not the same as regular bleach.

Electrical

Do you hear buzzing around your electrical outlets? Have you ever noticed the lights flickering on and off in any one particular room? Well it's good that you have noticed it because now you can do something about. I won't get into too much about electrical maintenance, simply because it needs to be done by a professionally trained electrician. It would be irresponsible for me to give information that might encourage you to get brave and fix things yourself. By now you know what to look for around your house. If you find anything that shows signs of aging or some deterioration, you simply call your licensed electrical expert and have them look into that for you. If you see flickering lights or you hear buzzing coming from a plug or outlet or fixture, then you know that you may have a loose connection in there and it would simply need to be investigated as the connectors may need to be tightened and if it's a case of using a copper outlet or fixture with aluminum wiring, then that may need to have some aluminum anti-oxidant applied on the connector.

Test your ground fault plugs (usually in any room where there is a water source within about three feet from the plug) often to see if they do shut off when they need to. They usually have a "test" button on them for that. Of course after you've tested them to see if they shut off, you can turn them back on.

Oh and before I forget, try not to connect too many things unto an extension cord that's plugged into one plug. To you it may seem like you are giving yourself another free outlet to plug in your TV, sound system, game console and whatever else, but in reality it's like...and I don't know if you've ever done this but sometimes you want to eat until you feel full right? Well apparently according to a Confucian philosophy still practiced by people in Okinawa Japan, you should only eat until you are 80% full. It's supposedly because it often takes your stomach about 20 minutes to communicate with your brain on just how full it is and if you keep eating until you feel full, you've probably already over eaten after all. I'm not a diet coach or anything but I just found that fascinating and now you know this too. Before eating, they would say:

"Hara Hachi Bu"

Which essentially translates to eating until you are only 80% full.[3] So when you plug multiple things to an outlet (or even worse if you decide to connect one extension cord to another extension cord and then plug all those used outlets into one wall outlet), irrespective of how many safeguards you may or may not have like an electrical breaker or an arc fault breaker in the panel, you likely will be loading too much on your electrical circuit which causes some overheating. If you do this long enough and hopefully your electrical breaker just trips off and shuts off. In the worst case scenario, you could literally be playing with fire.

Heating

I want you to think about your heating system as being at least as important as your car. Sure it won't cost you nearly as much as it costs to buy a new car but don't forget when I told you earlier about just how important your heating system can

---

[3] https://en.wikipedia.org/wiki/Hara_hachi_bun_me

be especially in the winter time. In a cold Canadian climate your heating system is keeping you alive. Just as you need to be aware to change your motor oil every five thousand kilometers on your car, you should look into having your ducts and your furnace cleaned at least once a year and ideally around spring time when the transition is being made from summer to winter. This will just simply give your furnace the best chance of surviving the full length of its expected useful life. Don't get me wrong, when a furnace has reached the end of the road then it's time for it to be replaced so you don't have a mid-winter shut down. Just care for your furnace so that it can keep you warm for a long period of time.

If you have a thermostat, you may notice a warning on it when the battery is getting low especially if it's a digital one. If it's not digital and you don't have any way of knowing, you can simply look to replace it every six months or so. Most thermostats have a front compartment that simply clips unto the wiring that's mounted on the wall so carefully pull out the front compartment and behind it, you should see where the battery goes and use the same kind of batteries as are there right now.

By now you have learned many valuable asset saving tips but I still want to give you some more advice. Now that you know what to look for and what sort of maintenance you need to do to protect your biggest investment, the question now becomes what happens if renovations need to be done to rescue my asset?

Well I will go into some detail about how to hire contractors and keep everyone on the same page. Hey, you may even save some money in the process of following my advice.

CONTRACTORS

It's as if contractors these days have gotten a bad rep from individuals who have given house owners a bad taste in their mouths. Truth is, and if you actually look at this objectively, in any industry you will have good and bad apples. And honestly some (not all) of the problems that come up between owners and contractors is simply miscommunication. You may think you're saying one thing but they're hearing something completely different. I remember this very clearly how once I was talking to a friend of mine, who now lives in the United States and he was ranting off about how he didn't understand why his lady was mad at him. She had come home complaining about some failed communication with someone at work and when he gave his 2 cents, she flared up at him and got mad. When I asked him a little bit more, he said something about her saying something to the colleague who took it the wrong way and now she was second guessing how she said it.

When I asked Jamie what he said in response, he said:

"Well I said - that was stupid -. She wanted my opinion and I gave it to her honestly"

And then he wonders why she got mad at him. Firstly, just because she was venting didn't mean she needed his advice and secondly and more importantly, it was all in his delivery. Hey I'm all for authentic expression but there are ways to get your point across. I told him that he could have said the same thing to her but in a different way and he would have gotten a completely different reaction. Instead of saying, "that was stupid", he could have easily told her, "well, how would you feel if someone said that to you?" Or "well you've said it and you can't take it back. Best you can do is put your ego aside and tell her simply that your intention was to say this instead and leave it be." That's still authentic expression I mean if his goal was to butt heads with her then I would have said, "Hey. Let the cards fall as they may" but by his rant, I'm guessing that wasn't his intention. Truth is she could have still gotten mad at him if he said what I suggested but I know that depending on delivery, it's easy to miscommunicate even though we're speaking the same English language.

Now imagine you wanted to have a brand new wraparound deck built and attached to your house and you tell your contractor that. You describe how it will wrap around and it should have railings for safety and then you pay the contractor to get some materials to do the job. You go to work and come back home not really thinking about it. The next day you go to work before the contractor gets there and when you come home, you decide to come into the house on the side where your wraparound deck is being built and what you see doesn't match what you saw in that magazine. Here's where the problem comes in. You said you wanted a wraparound deck and the contractor built you a wraparound deck but now the stairs are coming in on the right side when facing the house from the back instead of straight ahead. You wanted the deck to come out oh about 5 or 6 feet from the house so you can have multiple guests walking around on the deck with ease of movement. What he built was a deck that came out only about 3 feet. It was more of a landing than a deck.

"is he serious right now? How could he not see what I showed him?"

You may think to yourself. Now there's a disagreement between you and the contractor because for one, they've put in hours and would definitely want to be paid and secondly, the work would likely have to be redone. On top of that you either have to pay for what's been done only to have it redone or you refuse to pay and if the contractor is disgruntled enough then they may put a lien on your house. In this case, the contractor did nothing wrong. You simply did not communicate your ideas clearly enough. The contractor may or may not be a family man but they have obligations. They're people too and so when anyone starts to paint all contractors with the same brush of potentially being dishonest, then let's at least agree that that assumption is ignorant and emotionally motivated, not based on facts. Now let's get into my advice on how to successfully deal with contractors.

Hiring/selection process

You can find contractors on kijiji, craigslist, ask friends and family or even go to your local hardware store between 7 a.m. and 9 a.m. That's usually when the guys are loading up their materials for the day. You just want to get their cards and tell them you'll call them later to ask questions about the work you want done. You don't really interview them at this time.

When you have a few names, you can call them up and ask questions. There are many important questions that you could possibly ask like liability and all that but I'll tell you about the ones that I focus on over and above the obvious.

• **Ask about how long they've been in business for.**

You obviously want someone with experience doing what you want done but keep in mind that you may have someone who says they've had their company for a year or six months but if you dig deeper, they've been in the business for over fifteen years, working for someone else. They have the experience but only broke out on their own recently which could be a benefit to you because the person just starting out on his or her own may be willing to negotiate better in your favour so that they can build that volume.

• **Ask them what their specialty is.** It's not uncommon for a contractor to know how to do most things. When people start in construction, it's not uncommon that they started with doing one particular skill. It's also common for a contractor to have people in his or her crew who can do whatever work it is that you want. The point is to make sure that the person doing the work has experience or has direct access to the right person. You wouldn't want someone rewiring your whole house and the only experience they have is from reading a manual would you?

• **Ask them to tell you about a job they did where they had to go back for whatever reason.** Now this is a very good question because in construction, you may have to go back to a job even if it wasn't as a result of bad workmanship. Now it doesn't happen often at all but if someone tells me they've been in business for over fifteen years and they've never had to go back for any reason, I get curious. Most times when you ask that question, the contractor may become just a little defensive saying stuff like, "oh well...the client changed their mind" or "they went ahead and painted over the drywall mud before it was dry even though I told them not to just yet". That sort of response doesn't bother me because I know that sometimes clients can be unreasonable and I also know that things just happen. The purpose of the question is firstly to see how forthcoming they are for no one is perfect and secondly, how did they handle it.

• **Ask the contractor if they have their own vehicle and their own** tools as well as who they have access to for work that is outside of their skill level.

• **Feel free to ask any other questions** although I would say asking for a quote over the phone may not always be the best. There are always multiple factors that make no two projects really identical and the contractor should want to see the work that needs doing.

Reference checks

I usually ask for at least four references of work they've done in the past and I want one to be for a job that they had to go back to for whatever reason.

When I call the references, I want to know about how the work was, I want to know about how the experience was and I want to know how this contractor interacted with the homeowner throughout: did they keep the owner in the loop as to what's going on? (not play by play but let them know what's going on), how did they handle changes in the work as they came along? Stuff like that.

Oh and there's one thing I do with every reference. So say the contractor told me that he completely renovated John's main floor kitchen, what I would do is I would say:

> "Forgive me but I think I have my notes mixed up. I think he said that he did the tile in the bathroom or something?"

And let them talk. On more than one occasion, the contractor's reference went along, agreeing with me on the work that I suggested may have been done. Hey buddy! There goes that contractor. If the person on the reference corrects you and tells you just what it is the contractor had told you they did for them, then you know that this is most likely a real customer and not just some friend of his or hers whom they told to wait by the phone and give a good reference.

Finally, I ask the reference what the contractor could have done better to make the experience seamless. The purpose of this question is for me to be aware in dealing with the contractor not so much for me to discard the contractor from my list of prospects.

Quotes

Unless you have a contractor that you absolutely trust one hundred percent because they're family or they were referred by someone whose judgement you absolutely trust, I advise you to get multiple quotes on the work to be done. I'd say get at least three quotes for the same job. If possible, I want you to make sure each contractor giving a quote is giving a quote for the same description. If possible, write it all down so that they're quoting the exact same job. More on this shortly.

It's very common that the quotes will be different but I wouldn't automatically just go with the lowest quote just yet. When asking the contractors to give you a quote, ask them to break the quote down by labor and materials. They may be able to and they may not be able. If they do, then you can objectively see the numbers at that point. Now assuming that you got them to quote on the exact same thing, then you can make your decision from there. You don't want to go with the lowest quote only to find out that you omitted something in your description and then they do what they quoted you, only for you to have to cross that bridge when you get to it. They'll have to charge you more to do that extra component you missed out the first time.

Even after you have quotes, see if the contractor might consider adjusting their quote a little since you'd like to go with them. Many times if they're the lowest and you don't have any other quote to show that their price is really competing with someone else, they may not go for it but what do you really have to lose anyways? Feels awkward to ask them that? If you don't want to be all "negotiatee" (how I came up with that word I don't know but stay with me here) simply say something like:

> "Hey I feel very comfortable going with you for this work but first I wanted to know if there's any way you could help me on the price without really digging into your pocket."

You never know, they just might. Hey maybe if it works and you save a few hundred bucks, you can go ahead and buy a couple of extra copies of this book to share with someone you care about.

On the topic of quotes, sometimes you might save some money getting the materials yourself rather than having the contractor get it for you. Its really not uncommon for a contractor to charge you for their time and gas money or even a slight markup to go pick out all your materials. It's funny I was talking to my wife the other day and I was telling her that whenever I go to Home Depot and I'm getting more than one item, I'm sure to spend at least a half hour in that store and that's just for little items. As if I don't other things to do in my day. If you want to take the time and have the means to do it, go for it.

Personal vibe/connection

When you have contractors come out to give you a quote, you want to pay attention to how they interact with you as a person. Do they take off their shoes when they come into your house? (to be fair, if your house is not exactly conducive for a stranger to feel comfortable or safe walking around in socks, then I wouldn't take off my shoes either) Do they come smoking and drinking some coffee and they leave behind the coffee cup or the cigarette butt? Have you ever thought about the distinction between paranoia and intuition? With paranoia, you already have preconceived notions about something and that automatically sets the tone for your interactions. You assume most contractors are out to get you and when everyone comes out, to you its about finding out who wants to get you the least. Well with intuition, you are simply going about your day and you take things as they come. If someone shows up and you have a series of interactions that you're not sure of, then you simply make a mental note of it. They showed up smoking and maybe they came in your house still smoking or something, you take a mental note. I'm not asking you to go all psychic here. Just pay a little attention because leaving a cigarette butt on your front step just might be a sign of what you'll see when your house becomes their job site in the future.

Scope of work

This is usually the part where problems are stopped even before they start. Remember the scenario of the contractor building you a wraparound deck earlier? This is where you want to have it addressed. If you want your whole living room painted, you need to state that you want the ceiling painted this colour and in this sheen, you want the walls painted this colour and in a minimum of two coats and you want the trim painted in this colour and this sheen. Now do you see how that is different from saying, "I want to paint this room all this colour and then maybe paint the ceiling this colour as well". When you're describing it, it could be mostly general but you want to be as specific as possible in the scope of work. Yes, it can be a pain especially if you are having multiple projects to do around the house but hey, that's what you have to do to prevent miscommunication. Take your time and look at just about every component in the room where you want work done. If you want curtain rods put up, think about exactly how you want it to look and then describe it (as close to the ceiling as possible, about five inches out on either side of the window trim, etc.) You can go to www.re-peters.com/yourhousebonuses to get a free sample of a scope of work that I use as part of your resources.

Payment

Okay this one is something that you will have to discuss with your contractor because it has to be fair for everyone. If your contractor will be getting the materials, they likely will require a deposit. Since they will be purchasing things for your house out of pocket, it is only fair to show your commitment to the project. Just as homeowners have been burned, so have contractors. They order and pay for all this stuff and then the customer changes their mind? No thanks. So yes a contractor may ask for a deposit especially if they will be picking up the materials. Typically, its between five and thirty percent when I deal with contractors. If you're the one getting the materials, then I don't see why you should have to pay a deposit. I once had a contractor ask for fifty percent up front and I just kept it moving. I'm buying the materials and you want how much? Next! The goal here is for you to be reasonable. If you know that you don't want to run around Home Depot, trying to either find the right aisle or find someone who will direct you to the right aisle, only for you to get there and their shelf is empty so now you have to find someone who is qualified to get the right equipment to go up and get you what you need...and then you go to the next thing on your list and try to find it, then let's be reasonable (can you tell I was ranting a little?) if you don't want to deal with all that then hey, give the gal or guy a break. They're doing what it is that you don't want to or cannot do yourself.

Here's something I tell clients about payment. Usually, contractors are not always big fans of this especially the smaller company guys but when you make an agreement and the job is larger, you want to break it down into draws. When this, this and this is completed, you pay this much. The part that some contractors are not usually comfortable with is a holdback. You always want to hold back a certain amount until the work is 100% complete. So many people have run into situations whereby the contractor asks for full payment when they were 80 – 90 % done and then the contractor either didn't show or suddenly wasn't doing the work with as much zeal: dragging the renovation out. What incentive would they have after all, they've been paid in full. I typically hold back 25% or more depending on the size of the job. Again, if someone is installing kitchen cabinets that's one thing but if they are redoing the roof, flooring, windows, bathroom and kitchen, then that's a sizeable job. What you don't want is for this person to skip town on you only for you to hire someone else to finish the job. Needless to say it ends up costing you a lot more in the end.

Ready To Sell?

W ow. We have come a long way together, getting to know your house and your needs. As I promised when we started, by the end of this book I want you to have the confidence to look at your house and know that whatever it is you need to deal with, you can handle it. So now let's get into this aspect if you decide to sell your house.

When you decide to sell your house, hopefully you've been able to maintain it or bring the house to be in its best possible shape for you to get the most out of your investment. Let me tell you all about what you can expect the process to look like when it's time for you to sell your house. So here, instead of being overwhelmed, I will walk you through the complete experience.

BEFORE THE SALE

If you want to make the best of your biggest investment and it is time for you to sell, I want you to really consider having your house put its best foot forward. You will get only one shot to make a good first impression. If your house is in top shape that will happen naturally. A buddy of mine told me once about some study done at Harvard University about first impressions and social interactions and they gave an analogy of going for a job interview in a sweat suit or going in a business suit or shirt and tie. I can see how that would be relevant for some jobs I mean you could be the best at what you do but if you were going to get a job say as a lawyer's assistant or something and you showed up to the interview in sweats, well you're not doing yourself any good. Even if your house is really up to snuff, you just may give off the wrong vibe to potential buyers. Okay, let's get into this.

Here are the top four ways to give your house its best appearance:

1. <u>Clutter</u> –Too much stuff in a room makes it hard to imagine how to use a room. It also makes a room look small and crowded. Remember it's your buyer who has to like the house in order for them to buy it. Address this by clearing as much stuff from the house before showing it to potential buyers.

2. <u>Completely empty house</u> – It has been my experience, in all cases staging a house gives it a much better look than leaving it completely empty. When people walk through an empty house, it just feels like four walls rather than a home. In some cases, that may not be such a bad thing but then it happens often where buyers are

walking through a house, trying to place their furniture as they go through each room and they come to a room in the house and they don't know what to use it for. "Well that's wasted space" they might think as they would be uncertain it could work for their needs. If you are present when they say that, you could show them what to use the room for but many times you're not and you don't want to leave it to them. Truth is that many buyers do not have that foresight to be able to tell what to do with some spaces in a house.

3. Cleaning – You want to make sure that your house is extra clean. Besides the obvious things to clean such as your floor and bathrooms and kitchen, make sure your windows are streak free, wash walls if you have to, rent one of those rug doctor things to clean your carpet or hire someone. Just clean the place up so that it looks and smells good. If you have pets, it would be advisable to clean thoroughly and, if possible, remove all signs of the pet from the house while showing it.

4. Staging – I have touched on staging before and want to highlight the essentials that staging provides as well as how that will be beneficial to you.

• **Painting** – This is one of the cheapest ways to give your house a nice, clean look. You will want to paint the house in neutral tones. One simple idea is to visit show homes whenever they have open houses to get an idea of the colors that are in style now. If you are thinking about selling, you want your buyer to like the color regardless of your personal preferences, so keep that in mind.

- **Wall coverings** – As much as possible, minimize personal photographs. You can put a couple here and there but consider hanging paintings on the wall. The goal is to make the walls not look too busy and also to give an aesthetic appeal. One way to do this is combining light, neutral colored walls with paintings that have a touch of color. It would even be nicer if you found say a couple of couch pillows or other accessories that have the same color as one of the colors in the painting to keep it simple, stylish and sleek.

- **Window coverings** – If you can, try installing your curtain rod to be only a couple of inches from the ceiling and also spanning about six inches over either side of the window width. When you put up your curtain, you can slide the panels to the end of the curtain rod and just outside of the window's full width giving your window a larger look.

- **Furniture** – You want to minimize the amount of furniture in each room. Only put enough furniture to show the potential buyer what that room is meant to be used for. If in your master bedroom, you have your bed, a book shelf, two dressers (one that your grandpa made by hand so it's an emotional piece), consider leaving just the bed and one dresser. The goal is to show what the room is for without crowding the room and buyers thinking its smaller than it actually is. Less furniture makes it look like there is ample storage in the house itself.

- **Kitchens and bathrooms** – Consider placing candles or small potted green plants (even if fake) around your window sills or on an end of the counter. You don't want it to be too busy. What you want is for the pop of color to catch the peripheral vision of your buyer. Plants and flowers have a mood boosting effect on people. They may not notice it but those subtle mixes of the right colors will add to the feeling of being at home. Also use clean towels to add color to the space. Just do not get too aggressive on patterns. Get a nice shower curtain that ties in the colors of the towels. Minimize the toiletries that are visible. You can leave a couple of toothbrushes in a holder on the sink and maybe a shampoo and conditioner on the side of the tub but that's it. Once again we are looking for a sleek and clean visual.

- **Dining room** – You can really make a dining room look more luxurious by simply placing a rug underneath the dining table and then placing a center piece in the center of the dining table. Consider a round glass bowl with white flowers arranged in such a way that it completely covers all of the top of the bowl to give a full look. Candles can also set an ambiance in the dining room.

- **Exterior** – When people pull up, the first thing they see is the front of the house. Paint the front door so it looks vibrant and welcoming, plant some cheap, drought resistant plants that have some color (you can never really go wrong with green), trim any wild looking trees or bushes. You could even spend a little bit on your house number sign. Depending on how the rest of the house looks and the color for the rest of the exterior of the house, you could just paint the front of the house to give it a fresh look (obviously you will want the paint color to at least complement if not match the other sides). It is very important to keep the lawn and yard cut, tidy and weed free. This makes a nice and presentable first appearance.

Following those steps should get you set to give your house a good impression. If you need to get more in depth advice on staging, or want someone to help with the finer points, you can contact a local staging company.

You can also visit: www.cashbuysyourhouse.ca/ask-the-experts and ask our experts for more information.

Now your house looks just right for people to start coming through the door. Wait. Before you start rolling that ball down the hill, there's something I want you to do for me...well it's for you really not for me. I'm wondering, why are you selling?

As you answer that question within yourself, there's something I want you to do: I want you to go get a pen and paper...I'll wait.

Have one? Alright so I have a little bit of homework that you must do and the purpose of doing this is to really clear things up in your mind. This clarity will be key as you make many smaller decisions later on throughout the process of selling your house. You will write three specific things, ready?

Okay so I'm wondering, what's the story that has brought you to this decision? Go ahead. Take the time to write it out in about five sentences...are you finished with that? (You can take a little more space if you need to). What has changed?

Next, write out what you look forward to in your life after the sale of your house. It could be you sitting on a beach with clear blue water, or you having that feeling of the proverbial weight being lifted off your shoulders or it could just mean you moving back to the country. Whatever it is, it's something that the sale of your house will allow you to do. I don't know what that looks like but I want you to write it all out now.

The final piece of this homework, after you've written your story with the house up to this point and you've written out what life after the sale you'd like, I want you to write down a number. This number is very important. What the heck is this number? This number is a price that you know will realistically get you from the where you are now, to the positive new chapter after the sale of your house. This is not a number you hope you will get in your wildest dreams but instead, the minimum you will need in order for you to say in hindsight, "You know what, I'm glad that I was able to get X amount because now I can do this and that." You get my point. The purpose of you coming up with your minimum number is twofold:

First of all, when it comes time to sell, you will need this in your negotiations so that you know what your absolute bottom line is whereby anything lower and you're going to be walking away from the discussion. Remember a time when you may have been driving or someone you know may have been driving and then they caught themselves because their muscle memory was taking them in a total different albeit familiar direction? When the time comes, if you're not clear on what you're doing, you will very likely be reacting on a whim to everything and anything that will come up that's why we're going through this process together right now. So that when the time comes, you remember what you are doing it for.

The second reason is because when you figure out what your number is, you can compare that with what you can realistically get for your house in the current market at the time. This way you may be pleasantly surprised to see that there is the possibility for you to get what you want and more, or it just may be that the current market or even possibly the condition your house is in, may not allow for you to get exactly what you realistically need in order to move on to the next phase in your life.

Listen to me. It's important that you do this exercise **before** the first pair of feet walk through that front door. I would advise you to be prepared so that you're not overwhelmed when the process really kicks in. Only you can address these three points and I hope you can be honest with yourself. If you need more paper, go ahead. This is really for you and no one else but you must take the time now to do this so put this book down for a couple of minutes. I'll be here when you get back. When you write something down, you are giving clarity to what's on your mind. Has this ever happened to you where you just can't seem to fall asleep at night? Now aside from medical reasons, even I have found that sometimes when I can't seem to fall asleep, it's simply because my mind is trying to sort through a million and one things in my head.

The interesting thing is that once you write down all the stuff on your mind, it puts everything in perspective. You may not have all the answers right away but it almost lifts all that from your mind and places it on the piece of paper. That moment of getting it down on paper is like a release and, I don't know about you but, my goal is to get some sleep. Truth is though that most times whatever was keeping me up at night wasn't something that I could do anything about until the morning anyway so I would just write it out and go to bed. The mind does have an interesting way of sorting things out and the fact is that the mind can actually only think of one thing at a time effectively.

Do you know your reason for selling now? You may be able to say why you're selling in one sentence now but can you see how this is much closer to your core than when you first answered that question in the beginning?

Showing your property to potential buyers

If your marketing efforts pay off, you will get some calls from people looking to come see your house. If you organize open houses, you may get people stop by to take a look. The first thing to know is that not everyone who is looking at your house will either be interested in or capable of buying the house. The last thing you would want would be for a couple to come by, take a look and then they request a second showing and during that time you overhear them say that they love the place. They go ahead and put an offer with a deposit of $1000 dollars. Okay that's not a strong deposit but it's still something but more importantly, they're offering to pay exactly what you want. You've begun to count the money in your head that you'll receive and you've figured out how you plan on spending it. Two weeks go by and at this point, you've turned down other interested parties because you have it in the bag, until you get a call. Apparently the bank refused to put the deal through but no deeper explanation than that. Well my friend, more likely than not, your excited and cute couple just could not afford it and so the bank would not approve the transaction. You'll of course have to return their deposit because it was within the period of conditions with their offer.

If you have someone show interest in your house, you can ask some simple questions about how long they've been looking and what's been missing in the other houses that made them hold off (you're gauging to see if your house has what they want or not but would probably still let them come by) and also ask them who they are pre-approved with and till when? Don't ask the potential buyer if they are pre-approved for a mortgage because they simply have to say yes without any thought. If you ask it the other way especially if the question just pops up, they will often respond from the hip and if they cannot come up with the name of a financial in stitution (or say they're paying cash, which is good) right away, then it's something to be aware of. Not a deal breaker, but just to be aware of. Don't put off other interested parties when you have a tentative offer. Many things can fall through and your house is still available for sale until an offer's conditions have been met and both parties have signed and agreed to everything.

You see, you want people to come by and see the house. As many people as possible, so let people in. Just let it also be on your time, within reason. If you work 12 hours a day and you only allow a two-hour window every day for people to possibly see the place, you are cutting down your potential buyers by a lot because as you know today, we're all busy and the chances of everyone's schedule lining up to your two-hour window is very slim.

If you choose to hold an open house then you should ideally have someone else there with you because if you have a few people come by, you want to be able to answer questions while the other person sort of greets guests and/or hands them information sheets.

GENERAL LEGAL STUFF

Disclaimer: Once again, I'm not a real estate lawyer so this is not exactly legal advice. This is simply me sharing with you what I have seen from actively doing several millions of dollars' worth of real estate transactions since 2008, giving you an idea of the process. You must consult with a real estate lawyer with any questions you may have about this legal stuff. You will need one for your real estate transaction anyway so you might as well initiate contact. Think of my advice as helping you come up with the right questions to ask your lawyer when you sit across their desk. If you don't know what to ask, you'll simply be reacting as things come up and I'm assuming that you, just like I, won't find it fun to be in a state of constant reaction to things popping up.

Okay so now that we've made it clear that this is not legal advice and that you will need to contact your lawyer for this process, I'll break this down into simple sections based on what you can expect once you have found a buyer and they are ready to put an offer in writing. These steps include; the negotiation, the offer, the processing period, when you start packing, and what happens after you hand over the keys. Are you ready to get started? Don't worry, as I said, I'll be your guide.

The Negotiation

One day, after all your hard work, an offer has come in. You will meet the buyer either at your house or somewhere else. Feel nervous yet? Don't worry. It's really not as crazy as you might be thinking right now. The bottom line in all this is that you will be prepared because of the homework that I asked you to do earlier (you did your homework right? If not, do it before this meeting for your sake). By now you should be clear on three things:

1. Your story up until the point when you decided it's time to sell (specifically pertaining to your   story   surrounding your house).

2. What you look forward to after the sale.

3. Your number (what you need from the sale) that will take you from this chapter of your life to the next.

Knowing those three things when you come to the negotiation table can very easily make all the difference between you moving on with your life or letting your ego hold you back and leave you stranded for months. Believe me when I tell you that if that happens and you've had to hold on to the house for a few months longer, don't be surprised if you start saying something like this to yourself:

"Oh man that offer that I turned down three months ago sure looks really good right about now."

By then, the people who come by the house to look would be wondering what was wrong with it since no one wanted it after all this time, which, in turn, opens the door for lowball offers. If you know the amount that you need to get from the sale, it's easy to distinguish between a win-win situation and one that's not. You should always ask for more than what you need from the sale because it gives you wiggle room for negotiation and you never know what others are willing to pay; don't sell yourself short. On the other hand, please, don't get greedy. If you feel your house is worth somewhere around a certain amount and you insist on getting $50,000 more than that amount just because you want that extra money without offering value, then you're just asking for it and quite frankly you deserve to have your house sit on the market a while. Just because you put in a golf putting green in your backyard and you spent $9,000 to make it look like something out of a magazine doesn't justify that kind of increase if the values in your neighborhood don't support that. Now if someone offered you $20,000 more and an appraiser gives the thumbs up or your buyer is an all cash buyer then hey, you got lucky but don't hold your breath.

Offer to Purchase

If you have a buyer make an offer and for whatever reason you are not sure about how to look through the paperwork (simply because sometimes the wording on legal documents can be a little interesting at times) you should be able to get professional opinion. I tried reading a book called *Canterbury Tales* which is an English Literature book once. Let me tell you, I don't remember struggling to read a book that much in my adult life: it was very dry and used a lot of old English references. Legal documents can have the same effect and if you're not too comfortable going through it, you do have it within your rights to have your lawyer look through the paperwork and explain it to you before you sign. Keep in mind that some buyers will insist that you make a commitment in that moment or they walk away. Now before you jump to the conclusion that that's a scare tactic some buyers use, let's look at it a different way. If you put your house up for sale, there is the assumption that you have thought about how much and how you want the transaction to go right? In addition to that, if a buyer has committed funds to give you what you want, I don't know about you but I wouldn't be interested in making an offer and have them dangling it around other buyers, hoping someone else might pay $500 to $1,000 more. If someone makes an offer and does not agree with you taking it to your lawyer to look it over first, you have a decision to make. If you really don't understand many of the items on the form then your only protection is having your lawyer look it over before you sign if you feel comfortable enough and don't want to lose that buyer, then you may sign it knowing that you are legally bound to the terms of that agreement.

> *Tip: A more proactive approach would be to look at some sample documents and possibly have your lawyer explain any sections you don't quite understand prior to meeting your buyer. There is still the chance that your buyer may not be using a standard agreement though*

Deposit

When your potential buyer gives you a deposit cheque, it's usually written out to the name of your lawyer's law firm. Your lawyer's firm usually has a trust account where they are required by law to hold on to the funds in accordance with the terms of the offer to purchase until all the conditions have been satisfied for your lawyer to give the buyer a clean and clear title of ownership on the house. Now I have seen situations where the sellers wanted some of that deposit money to move before the possession date. If that seems to be the case, your best bet may be to borrow some money to tide you over until you receive whatever lump sum remains after the sale and then you replenish your original source of funds. Okay so you and the potential buyer have discussed and verbally agreed to an amount. According to the real estate laws of CANADA in order to make an offer legally binding there has to be an exchange of consideration which generally is money. You can put down a minimum of one dollar in addition to both your signatures. One dollar is legally acceptable but ask yourself, if you were selling something on Kijiji say a TV for five hundred dollars and someone came by to put down just five bucks and told you to hold on to the TV and not sell it for a couple of months because they have to get a ride to come pick it up, what would likely be your thought? Meanwhile you have someone else who is willing to come and pick it up a day after and they're ready to buy it now. Which would you go with and why? The person who put down the five dollars may genuinely want the TV but that's not a very good show of faith. I've heard of several instances where someone put an offer in on a house and then they gave a deposit of three hundred dollars. For a house worth over a quarter million ($250,000) for example, where is the show of faith in that? You and I may have good rapport but unless you show me that you are ready and able, I'm not so sure that I would want to leave it to chance. A thousand dollars might be a show of seriousness so that if the person does walk away from the deal (and it has happened a lot), then you know that they are leaving some proverbial skin in the game. I don't know about you but it's not that difficult to walk away from a three-hundred-dollar deposit if the overall transaction is a commitment of six figures. But to walk away from three to five thousand dollars or more? Yeah I'm sticking around to see things through. Of course you always have a recourse if you enter into a legally binding agreement the proper way and the buyer decides to walk away from the deal. You could go through all that but the amount of time it would take and possible legal expenses for you to get a judgment in favor of you is just...I'm getting a headache just thinking about all that. Let's just agree that you won't put yourself through all that right? Unless you like more excitement in your life than usual in which case, all power to you. When your buyer puts a deposit cheque down, be aware if its a personal cheque that needs five to ten business days to clear. That could tie up your property for that long because you're legally bound with your signature and then that cheque could very well bounce. Whatever form of payment the buyer uses, you want to make sure that your lawyer can get access to that money right away to be put in a trust account

General Conditions of the Agreement

Once the deposit has been placed in your lawyer's trust account, any other conditions (financing, house inspection, other inspections) will usually be addressed during this time and these conditions usually have to be addressed within a reasonable amount of time from when the offer is accepted by you on paper. It's not uncommon that if a buyer has these conditions that are required by them, they would put in writing that these conditions will be met within a fixed amount of days of when the offer is accepted. There are no hard and fast rules for how long this process takes and it's not uncommon that a buyer may need an extension for some of the conditions or just write down conditions that could take a couple of weeks to address. If your potential buyer requests an extension, it's fair to grant an extension if the reason for the request to extend the timeline is found reasonable by you. These conditions that are requested by the buyer, give the buyer an out from the legal agreement if the conditions aren't met. As an example, if your house has a foundation problem and the buyer puts an offer for a certain price and it is subject to a foundation specialist inspecting the house and giving a satisfactory report, then when the foundation specialist comes out, they take a look and report to the buyer. The buyer may opt out because what the specialist discovered was requiring far more intensive work than the buyer had anticipated OR the buyer may come to you to go back to the negotiation table to address this issue. In either case, the buyer does have an out in that scenario. So once again, the buyer puts an offer (with deposit to your lawyer with a good minimum amount), the buyer may put in some conditions that they need satisfied in order for them to carry on with the transaction (and they are legally able to pull out of the deal if those conditions aren't met without breaching the agreement). The key here is that if a buyer has conditions that need to be met, you as the seller would want to know relatively quickly as to whether or not this is still going through. I hope you can imagine the level of excitement you might experience if the buyer put an offer with a possession date for a month away. You've packed all your things and moved to the new location only for you to hear a week before possession that the buyer cannot secure a mortgage to buy your house or some other issue. My guess may be as good as yours as to just how much of a headache that would be. As if we don't have enough stuff going on in our lives. In the event that the buyer's conditions are not met, your lawyer is to return the deposit amount back to their lawyer without any deductions for whatever reason unless otherwise stated in the written contract. If the buyer had given a cheque of three thousand and five hundred dollars, then a cheque for three thousand five hundred dollars should be returned back to the buyer. Provided that the buyer's deposit cheque did not bounce in the first place

Once the conditions laid out by the buyer have been met, then you can actually start getting ready to move on with your life because at this point, both you and the buyer are fully and legally locked into this agreement. All the things that you had highlighted in your homework I gave you earlier, are now well within your reach. It's time to pack your bags.

Here are some things I want you to be aware of courtesy-wise when you decide to move on. Unless the buyer specifically asked for some things that are not physically attached to the house (like a lawn mower or that old tube TV) do you and them a favor and clean your stuff up will you? If you don't, it is actually possible for the buyer to come after you through your lawyer for cleaning up any mess left behind. Unless it is explicitly agreed upon during the writing of the offer, then cleaning up your house of extra stuff is your responsibility. Also things like utilities and insurance are still your responsibility up until the day of possession as agreed upon in the original offer (or in writing if its mutually agreed upon to change).

The Finish Line

Now the date of possession is here. Call your bank and tell them you're coming in with a big cheque. Actually I was just kidding. That's not usually how it works. Between the time you signed the agreement and the date of possession, your lawyer is supposed to have been working on any and everything pertaining to making it easy for the buyer's lawyer to transfer ownership title from your name to the buyer's name. Any liens (contractor or private lenders are the two most common) that were on the title would need to be cleared up. Usually before the date of possession, the buyer's balance of payment should have been received by your lawyer and so they would have cleared everything out that's outstanding on your ownership title and then give a clean slate before you get your money. So this is how the process works as far as who gets paid what:

Any mortgage on the house is paid off (to the bank or whatever lender you had)

Any outstanding utilities (sometimes back taxes)

Any liens (to contractors or private loans or other judgements on your property)

Your lawyer's fees

THEN whatever is left over is released to you.

> *Tip: If you wanted to know how much you owe and what judgements there are on your title of ownership, you should be able to perform a search in an office in your area called a land titles office. You may have to pay very small fee to access that information but it is accessible. Alternatively, you can have your lawyer pull a title document on your house and that should have all that information.*

Depending on the jurisdiction where you live, you may get your money within a business day or so and sometimes, it can take about two weeks from the date of possession to the date that you would be able to get any funds coming to you from the sale. In some situations, it may take longer depending on how backlogged the folks are at the property registry office. Speak to your lawyer about how the process works in your part of Canada. Even in jurisdictions that take a couple of weeks after possession for you to get your money, there may be provisions that allow you to get the money much sooner (e.g. Western Conveyancing Protocol)

That seems like a lot to take in all at once and I know it can be daunting, especially if you have not done this before. You can get a simple checklist of steps to take through the selling process online at:

www.re-peters.com/yourhousebonuses. Following the steps I have outlined should see you through the process without additional stress and surprises. From staging, negotiating and a general idea about the legal process, make sure you are positioning yourself to make the transitions with ease.

CHAPTER 6

Selling As-Is

Now if your house is in tip-top shape that's fine. You can go ahead and try to sell the house yourself especially if you identify as a handsy homeowner, keeping in mind that it doesn't always work out when people try to sell their houses themselves. I mean if we could do every single thing, we would fix our cars, grow our own food, make our own clothes, and even build our own houses from the foundation up. My point is that selling a house can work for some. Hey, who can argue with a house that's got new windows, new custom kitchen cabinets, granite countertops, and all that. For many more people, it may not be so straight-forward. What if your house still needs work?

Let's say the house requires a lot of repairs, you have decided that you would rather be an overseer or solutions homeowner and would rather sell, and you know your three main points of focus (see the homework you did that I assigned to you earlier). What's next? Are you supposed to wait and hope it will be fixed somehow?

Well, you do have a couple of options that you can consider if you would like to sell your house as is. I'll explain that shorty. Some people would call such a house run-down or a fixer upper and by selling this way, you do not do the work. Let's think about some of the ways that you could sell your house, if it's in need of work, as is.

Real Estate Agent

Selling your house with a real-estate agent is certainly a valid option but usually if it's already fixed up. In addition, selling your house with a Real Estate Agent is usually best suited if you identify as an overseer type homeowner. As with all the options I'll be telling you about, I want us to look at both sides of the argument for each option together, and then the decision is yours – okay?

A real estate agent is a person licensed to buy and sell real estate and can help you market your house. In exchange, when your house sells, traditional agents typically collect a commission of about 5% of the total sales price. Non-traditional agencies may collect a fixed fee. The amount is paid by you – the seller– from the sales proceeds. Let's look at the different aspects of what to expect when you deal with a real-estate agent as you decide to sell your house.

Firstly, a good real-estate agent should be able to help you push the marketing of your house so you don't have to worry about that. If you're going to be paying 5% of the sales price of your house (which will usually be paid out after the mortgage and everything before you get what's left), there has to be some value, right? Well some but not all real-estate agents can be worth their weight and even more in gold: they truly have that hustle. As opposed to trying to market the house yourself, a good real-estate agent should do the research, know the trends and local street prices, and be able to take care of the marketing for you.

In fact, I think its best we look at the pros and cons for each of your options because then you can see things a bit more objectively, do you agree?

Pros

• ***A real estate agent will handle the marketing of your property.***

A good real-estate agent should help put your property out there. From the Multiple Listing Service (MLS), to digital advertisements, and maybe even door to door flyers. Each real estate agent is different and I know of realtors who are simply content with just sticking their sign in front of your house, and I know some who go above and beyond that to doing online ads, newspaper ads, and so on.

• ***A real estate agent can help you identify qualified buyers as well as guide you through the sales process.***

Not everyone who wants to or comes to take a look at your house is a qualified buyer. Your real estate agent should be able to ask the potential buyer or their agent the right questions to determine if the buyer is qualified. (I gave you some advice earlier on how you can go about this yourself if you choose to be a handsy house owner and sell your house on your own.)

• ***A real estate agent can help you spot any fishy business in the transaction.***

This is usually identified in the paperwork. Sometimes, just sometimes, you may come across a potential buyer who writes an offer, and they would have something in the write-up that could work against you. A real estate agent may be able to help you identify paperwork anomalies. Then again, you will be hiring a real-estate lawyer anyways, and your lawyer is the best person to look out for your legal interests.

You can also ask the buyer to go through every aspect of the offer with you before you sign. If you are unfamiliar or still uncomfortable, there's nothing wrong with asking that your lawyer look it over before you put your signature on it. Remember I also gave the advice to have your lawyer walk you through a sample agreement so that you familiarize yourself before an offer comes in.

• *A real estate agent can help you figure out the value of your house.*

I'm guessing that by now, you would have seen multiple ads of different agents offering to give you a free home evaluation. Real estate agents will often do this for you for free. Still there's something about that you need to be aware of, and I will be talking about it in the cons section.

Cons

• *A free market evaluation.*

Okay, so here's how this process works. Typically, an owner would have a free market evaluation from one or more real estate agents. They should all be coming up with just about the same price, right? Real estate agents have different ideas about how to stand out, and one tactic that came to my attention is an example of this. Some agents talk a sweet game about getting you more money on your house, and may show you past sales that make their argument sound plausible.

Now wait a minute – their value comes in much higher than the others who gave free evaluations. Why? Well one of the reasons – there are many, but here is one I've heard many times from people wanting to sell their house: an agent talks about the house just a street over being sold for "oh, about three hundred thousand dollars more" than you were thinking. Well, that could be a partial fact.

The question is, are the two houses identical in an apples-to-apples comparison? The house on the next street could be on a lake, or it could be twenty-five years newer than yours or have a new three-car attached garage while yours has a single detached, very old garage. My point is that on face-value – and with someone singing a sweet song to your ear – it may sound good, and if you're not objective in your approach, you'll be the one to deal with the consequences in the end.

- *Pricing a house to win the listing rather than according to the market.*

Back to this idea of selling you on a higher number because obviously that would make one agent's pitch more attractive to you than the others. It might sound something like:

"You know what, let's try this price for a couple of weeks, and if we don't get enough action we can adjust the price."

Part of this strategy, as I understand it, is that the goal of pricing at a good number is to win the listing over other realtors. If the house doesn't sell right away, the agent keeps adjusting (this means lowering) the price. The challenge posed to you is that if you come out of the gate with the wrong number, the market may not take it. Don't get me wrong, I'm guessing that it sometimes works. You can also throw some spaghetti at a wall and it could stick sometimes. If you do list too high and the market doesn't take it, you can lose your first wave of buyers early on.

If you miss that first wave of buyers, other buyers coming in may question the value of your house. "What could be wrong with this house that it's not sold by now?" is the sort of question other buyers may ask themselves if your house hasn't sold after a while. The price reductions I see average ten thousand dollars at a time – could be more. After a couple of weeks, don't be surprised if the agent brings up the conversation to lower the price in order to get more people to come through the door.

- *Real estate agents most often are looking for a buyer.*

They're looking to find you a buyer for your house and are not buyers themselves. Some real estate agents make the claims that they will buy your house if they don't sell it on the MLS. I'm not discrediting those claims because I've never tried their services but hey, something for you to be aware of. My point is that typically, a real estate agent won't be buying your house but instead looking for a buyer out there for you.

- *Having your neighbors and everyone else walk through your house.*

This is a big one that my clients have expressed concern about in the past. You see, when your house gets listed, a real-estate agent will try to give your house some exposure. This includes a sign in front of your house, and sometimes also signs on the street corners near you. Most people don't want random strangers – and especially not the neighbors they know – walking through their house if the house is being sold as is and needs renovations.

- *How long your house stays on the market.*

Now it's not uncommon for you to hear a real-estate agent say, "oh don't worry, your house will sell just like that." Unless they have a crystal ball or a real buyer for you, and connect you with a buyer right away, I'm not sure how this can be said with such certainty. It's a bit like expecting the weather person to forecast a one hundred percent chance of rain or snow. If it sells right away, then great but what if it doesn't? I'm wondering, how long will it actually sit on the market especially if its in need of repairs?

• ***You may need to fix a few things before putting your house on the market.***

You know, this argument is very fair and I'll say the same thing to you: if you want to get absolutely top-dollar for your house, then you will need to fix your house to the point where it's competing directly with houses that have new windows, custom kitchen cabinets, granite, new furnace, and so on.

You see, those things do have to be done and someone must fork out the money to do them. It will either be you or your eventual buyer. So yes, you could fix those things. The thing is, you shouldn't have to. You just have to know that no one (well no-one in their right mind) will pay a brand new price for a house that needs a laundry list of repairs done. I'm saying after all, that you don't have to fix all those things on your house. There are ways that you can sell it as is. We'll get to that.

• ***Scheduling viewings.***

Whether you try to sell your house by placing a Wal-Mart sign in front or you use a real-estate agent or even use a service like Comfree, you will have to make yourself available for people to come see your house. Now I'm not saying take a sabbatical from work to accommodate showings but you will be inconvenienced a bit.

It commonly happens that you get notified there are people who want to come and see your house within an hour or two of the notification. If you get that notification what are you going to do – refuse because it's your special time? Well you want people to come through your house, right? So you have to make yourself available.

I would not advise that you sit at home when people come by to take a look at your house with an agent. It just makes potential buyers uncomfortable and they will rush away which really serves you no good. You don't have to go far but can instead just go sit in your car or go to the neighbor's house (of course with their consent). You have to leave the house every so often or only allow showings between certain times. This could seem structured to you though you'll be missing out on potential buyers with conflicting schedules.

You might be lucky if the house you are looking to sell is vacant. In that case, the issue of your schedule doesn't come up anymore because real-estate agents usually have lock-boxes that they'll put on your property and so if someone wants to go take a look, their agent would just have to notify your agent and all that.

In Summary

Now you can see that a real estate agent can help you with certain aspects of selling your house. At the same time, if your house is not in pristine condition, there can be some real pitfalls you need to be aware of that could have stressful, time-consuming and costly consequences if you prefer to sell your house as is and use a real estate agent.

I'm sure you're beginning to ask if there's a simple solution to selling your house without the usual stress, stretched time investments, and costs. Keep reading...

CHAPTER 7

The Simple Solution

So far I've told you about how you can go about rescuing your asset through different means, I've told you about the selling process if your house is in tip top shape and even if it still needs some renovations.

Now what would it be like to be able to sell your house as is, where is? What "as is, where is" means is simply that you get to make absolutely no warranties about anything going on with the house. So if the furnace is faulty, you can verbally tell the buyer but if they took the keys and the next day the furnace goes out, well they cannot come back to you for any of that. If the house has uncompleted renovations, you're not obligated to finish the renovations unless for whatever reason, you both agree to it in writing.

The system...

How it works is that there are some people out there who are in the business of buying properties in a state of disrepair. They come in, take a look at the house and they would buy the house even in that state. Sometimes they buy the house to tear it down and build something new, sometimes they buy in order to fix and sell or fix and then rent it out. There are several options that these firms have on what they would be doing once they buy your house in that state.

What is possible with this solution?

When a company buys your house as is, where is, it allows you to truly focus on those three things that I gave you for homework earlier. The reason I call it a simple solution is that it is a much simpler solution than dealing with all the hassles of being a handsy homeowner and trying to renovate the house yourself or being an overseer homeowner and dealing with contractors and spending potentially tens of thousands of hard earned dollars. You can certainly market the house yourself or you can try to hire a real estate agent who may be good...if your house was in tip top shape. Truth is they may or may not find you the right kind of buyer for what your house needs.

Yes, you can go through all that but what if there was another option that was as simple as you getting a cheque and then handing over the keys? I'm wondering, now that you know your story and you know what you look forward to in your life after the sale, what would it actually be like to just move on and be done? Yes, that can truly be a simple process but what am I not telling you? At this stage in your life, surely you know that nothing can really be too go to be true right? Well, fairy tale movies can be but this isn't one of them so what's the catch? There are things you will need to be aware of about this process and how it pertains to your situation so let's get into it okay?

SELLING YOUR HOUSE AS IS WHERE IS

Pros

- *You should be able to sell "as is, where is".*

When working with a reputable company that offers this service, you should be able to sell as is, which basically means that you no longer have to worry about any more renovation headaches or costs and you don't have to make any warranties about anything.

- *You should pay NO Real estate commissions.*

If this is a simple solution, you should not have to subtract an additional 5% from your sale price to pay real estate commissions as these companies are usually not real estate brokerages

- *Your lawyer can look over the forms before you sign.*

Firstly, the company buyer should be able to explain the different aspects of whatever forms they present to you so that you are all on the same page as to what you are agreeing to. If it all seems too convoluted for you then you should have the right to have your lawyer look it over before you sign. There can be exceptions whereby you seem to be going back and forth between a reputable company and some weekend warrior guy (someone who does this in their spare time, once or twice a year) or something. In that case, this company can either choose not to go ahead with your house or you will have to make your decision. You could also pre-empt this by having your lawyer walk you through a standard agreement so that you familiarize yourself with the documents before you meet with your buyer.

- *You can get cash in a little as 7 days.*

In some cases, you can get an all cash offer for your house and you can get it in as little as five business days (which, including the weekend, makes it seven days)

- *Your house should spend ZERO days on the market.*

Since you will be dealing with a company that is the buyer and not trying to help you find a buyer, then that buyer should be your final stop in this process of selling as is. This means that your house doesn't have to stay on the market for any period of time.

- *You don't have neighbors and lots of strangers walking through.*

This is one of the big reasons why people choose this service. You see what goes on in your life doesn't have to be everybody's business. If you list your house with a real estate agent in its current state, well you can only imagine how curious your neighbors will be and imagine how many people will be coming through an open house. Surely everyone has an opinion on everything these days even when it doesn't concern them. Selling it this way to a reputable company, you don't have to deal with any of that. The neighbors will just notice one day that there's a new owner.

- *You're not working with someone looking for a buyer but the actual buyer.*

One thing also is that when you work with a reputable company, they should be the buyer and not representing you the seller in order to find you a buyer.

- *You should be treated like a person not a number.*

This should go without saying but you just might be surprised. If you go to some government offices, you may be required to take a number and have a seat till your number is called after which you will be attended to. When its your turn to be seen, you are called out by your number. Now I'm not saying that in a government office you are treated like a number because they have to have some sort of system so there is order in how they help people. What I'm saying is that when you deal with a reputable company to help you with this, you don't need someone talking down on you or you leaving the conversation feeling like you were just that...a number. Don't you agree or am I just overthinking it?

- *You can have your legal/closing costs paid for by your buyer.*

This is not an absolute must but wouldn't it be a little icing on the cake if you want to call it that? Wouldn't it be great to know that not only will your house be bought as is but you can also take this to your lawyer and once the deal goes through, you don't have to pay for your lawyer's fees? Well it's completely up to the company person you deal with but hey, why not ask? If you don't ask you'll never know.

Cons

- *You won't be getting full retail price.*

If your house is in need of renovations, then someone will absolutely have to do those renovations and come up with the tens of thousands of dollars needed to bring your house to being good as new again. If it won't be you spending that on the renovations, then it's only fair that this company will need to account for that in the form of a discounted price especially if you won't be making any warranties about anything. If the plumbing fails a day after they take the keys, that won't be your problem anymore.

- *You may be dealing with someone who only does this on the weekend as opposed to an established company.*

I don't know what it is that you do for work or used to do for work but have you heard of a guy who fixes cars out of his garage on the side or something like that? Well hey, he might be a wiz at it and all that but now let me ask you this question a little more seriously. Let's say you have a health issue and you need to have it treated so a friend tells you about this lady who used to be a surgeon or something and they could treat you faster than if you had to be on the waiting list of a specialist...let that sink in. If you know the person that you are dealing with personally then hey at least there's some pre-existing connection (although if they're not actively recognized by their medical association...I don't know). If you deal with someone off the street and we're talking about your house here, well you decide. My point is that you must know to properly screen who you are dealing with because at the end of the day, this is not a TV you're selling here. This is your house.

- *This company or person is going to make money off your house.*

I want to ask you, at your job what would you do if you had responsibilities for not just yourself at home but others as well, and then you were approached by your boss who said:

> "Hey can you help us out? I'll need you to give us seven days a week of your time for the next couple of months. Now the thing is, we're really tight on funds so we won't be able to pay you for your time is that okay?"

As you answer that in your head I'm wondering, how would that impact not just you but the other people you're responsible for at home? I remember one of the engineers I work with telling me a story about an architect in the 70's who used to build lots of houses. According to the engineer, this architect's company barely made any profit on any of the houses but they sure made a fine product. Didn't take long for the company to go out of business. Now when you hear of a company going out of business, perhaps you think of a large, multi national company or something but what about the family owned grocery store? What happened to that family afterwards and the families of the workers? Yes, companies need to make some profit for their risk in buying your house "as is" just as you need to get paid to do work and provide a life for you and yours. What it all comes down to is the home-work I gave you. When you have clarity, you can very easily decide if it's a solution for you.

• *You might be taken advantage of in legal terms or confusing terminology in paperwork*

I'm sure there would be many other stories similar to this but, I heard a story once of a real estate investor who approached people facing foreclosure as that list was easily accessible. He offered to buy their house from them and they would somehow buy the house back from him over time or rent it from him of some other setup. The problem wasn't so much the idea as it was that when the smoke had cleared, these people realized they had signed over ownership of their houses without getting anything in return and they were legally bound at this point. When you work with a company, the person should explain the paperwork and if you're not sure then your lawyer should look it over. I remember hearing my mentor once say:

"Re' it's better to be on the ground, wishing you were on a plane than to be on a plane in the air, wishing you were on the ground."

It's your house. It's your choice.

Why it is a great option

"You can be the ripest, juiciest peach in the world and there's still going to be someone who hates peaches."

- Dita Von Teese.

Now that we've gone through all this talk about pros and cons and all that, maybe you are asking the question about why this is a good option for you. If your house is one of the best looking houses in the neighborhood and has either new features, then this kind of service will not be a good fit for you. In the same token, if your house needs different kinds of renovations and you were hoping to sell it with a real estate agent, the kinds of buyers that are typically on the MLS are buyers who are looking for something fixed up or something where they could perhaps do a little painting on the weekend or something after they move in. Depending on the laundry list of repairs that your house needs, it would not be a good fit for retail buyers either. Where does that actually leave you? You can either fix it up to top shape and then sell it or you could sell it as is and move on with your life.

The Elephant in the room

I will address some questions that are often in the back of people's minds whenever it comes time to sell their house as is and they are going to be dealing with a company. The goal of telling you about these is so that you can think objectively whenever you are dealing with someone who says that they are a capable buyer.

• *Have you heard about this company before?*

It is possible that you never even knew a company that buys houses as is existed let alone what the name of such a company would be. Has this ever happened to you before? I remember when I wanted to buy my first pickup truck for work, it was a 2003 Dodge Dakota. Before I decided that this was the model I wanted, I saw cars and trucks on the road but the moment I made that decision, it was like I started to see dodge trucks all over the place. Weird right? Well you may have not heard about such a company before simply because you either didn't know they existed or you weren't really at the point where you were ready to sell.

• *What associations does this company belong to?*

Does the company belong to any associations where you can independently check about this company without having to go through them? Stuff like the Better Business Bureau and such. These associations exist independent of the companies that are part of that association so information is not biased.

• *How do I know that they are not a fly-by-night company or person?*

Well just like the guy who fixes cars out of his garage, how would you know that a company is here to stay? For one, how long have they been around? Then check things like associations, online presence and feedback.

• *At what stage during renovations or packing can I decide to call this company?*

You may think that since you've already started a renovation you would want to finish that kitchen renovation before calling a company to possibly come and buy your house as is, well you don't. There are countless couples I have met whereby they started a bunch of renovations and life got in the way and they couldn't finish and that should not be an issue at all in the process (just like James from "Tale of Two Homeowners" in the introduction). As for packing and all that, you may need to do that if you wanted to list with a real estate agent but that's really not necessary if you're looking to sell your house as is.

• *Have they helped other people or is this their first go at this?*

I heard someone say this once and I found it to be curious. They said that there's nothing more convincing than on a busy day to walk by an empty restaurant, to convince you not to go in. I understood it to mean that there must be a reason it's so empty. If someone is just starting, that doesn't mean they are incompetent at all. When it comes to a company you want to deal with, have they helped others? Do they perhaps have testimonials, reviews or a client history?

• *How do you know that this company won't be taking advantage of you?*

I have already talked about this earlier in the pros and cons but yeah if you're not sure, have your lawyer look things over before you sign, simple. You can go with your gut when you are dealing with such a company but the bottom line is that your line of protection is with your lawyer. If you have a vibe, take it to your lawyer. And don't forget that you and your lawyer can do a dry run with the standard paperwork so you get comfortable with it.

• *How do you know that this company is serious about buying your house?*

When it comes to a real estate transaction, the real way to know if someone is serious about doing the deal is if they do at least a bit more than the bare requirement necessary. One dollar and both signatures is what you need to make a deal but can a person walk away from one or five hundred dollars if the trade-off is that they'll be on the hook for six figures? I would think cold feet could surely make that possible. Would you walk away from a few grand? I don't know. Maybe you could but I don't know that I can say the same thing for me. The bottom line is money talks and a serious company will put a deposit down and start making immediate progress into the transaction.

• *How long might this process take?*

You should be able to sell your house as is when you are ready. You usually can sell your house in as little as seven days but it can be thirty or sixty days. The point is to work together with your buyer.

• *Does this company have an office or are they mobile professionals?*

Not that there's really anything wrong with mobile professionals after all banks have mobile mortgage specialists who meet people wherever suits them to conduct business. That's the nature of change. I think its more of an old-fashioned thing you know? Nowadays people have full, long conversations back and forth via text (I can't understand that but that's just me) or you conduct certain types of business only by email (don't get me wrong about eBay). Of course its not all set in stone because if you have a disability and the building where you are to meet is not easily accessible or whatever very valid reason, there should be flexibility. It is more of an added assurance that the company you are dealing with is reputable.

Conclusion

Wow okay, so we've been at this for a bit. I've taken you on a journey about you and your house. Firstly, you've learned about what makes your house age, then what can happen if you neglect it. By now, you should be able to say for sure what type of owner you are, be it handsy, overseer or solutions. You also know about different things you can do to slow down the aging process. You've also learnt from me about how to go about hiring a contractor if you were going to do any renovations and then the process of selling. If it was unfamiliar to you prior to this book, you now know about selling your house as is. Don't forget to go to www.re-peters.com/yourhousebonuses to get the checklists for what to look for and also the selling process if you were going to sell. Also make sure you do that homework I gave you if you decide to sell. You can thank me later. By now, you have a lot more knowledge about the various aspects and you should have the confidence to do this from here on out. Oh and one more thing, I want you to do something for me. If you know anyone who can benefit from the information in this book, you can either order them a copy of they can go get a copy on Amazon as well. Don't forget

100% of the proceeds will be going to The Salvation Army for the first half a million copies sold.

ABOUT THE AUTHOR

Re' Peters believes that business is firstly about taking care of the people side of things. After that, everything else falls into place. To Re' family is important and so is your purpose in life and how you impact people's lives. We are all part of this universe which is a divine school: we're always learning.

He is CEO of CashBuysYourHouse.CA a division of Alpha Properties Inc., which is an accredited member of the Better Business Bureau for Northwest Ontario and Manitoba. Since 2008, he has been and still is in the business of helping people find a simple solution to their unique real estate needs. His company, CashBuysYourHouse.CA specializes in buying houses in disrepair from owners who are ready to move on but are not willing or able to first implement the needed repairs because they do not have the emotional or financial resources to do so. After they buy these houses, his teams then implement the necessary repairs to restore these houses back to or better than their former glory days thereby improving the lives and communities that they come in contact with. Re' has been involved in several millions of dollars' worth of real estate transactions. Re' is married to his wife of many years and they have three amazing sons and they currently reside in Winnipeg, Manitoba.

Re' has decided to give 100% of the net proceeds from the sale of this published book, to The Salvation Army for the first half a million copies sold.

To contact Re' Peters, please visit:

www.re-peters.com/contact

If you happen to be on the social media platform, Instagram or Facebook, I would love to see a copy of this book in your hands. You can simply put in the hashtag YourHouseYourChoice (#YourHouseYourChoice). Also feel free to follow me on Instagram @Re_Peters and add me on facebook.com/repeters0. Let's grow together.

And finally, if you or someone you know has a house that is in a state of disrepair, first of all, have them get a copy and read this book, then do the homework in chapter 5 and then you can contact CashBuysYourHouse.CA today. The process can be as simple as them receiving a cheque then handing over the keys.

Here are some of the benefits from working with Re' Peters and CashBuysYourHouse.CA:

- You can get CASH for your house.
- You sell your house as is, where is.
- You can sell your house in as little as 7 days.
- You don't pay any real estate commissions.
- You can take our forms to your lawyer to look it over before you sign.

- We can pay your legal/ closing costs (depending on jurisdiction, typically up to $1,500).
- Your house spends ZERO days on the market.
- You will be treated like a person: with respect.
- No need to have neighbors walking through your house, knowing your business.

Once again, contact CashBuysYourHouse.CA today if you are ready to sell as is and move on to the next phase of your life or if you have any questions for our experts visit www.cashbuysyourhouse.ca/ask-the-experts